OLD TESTAMENT MESSAGE

A Biblical-Theological Commentary

Carroll Stuhlmueller, C.P. and Martin McNamara, M.S.C.
EDITORS

Old Testament Message, Volume 13

1—2 CHRONICLES EZRA, NEHEMIAH

Céline Mangan, O.P.

Michael Glazier, Inc.
Wilmington, Delaware

First published in 1982 by:
MICHAEL GLAZIER, INC.
1723 Delaware Avenue
Wilmington, Delaware 19806

Distributed outside U.S., Canada & Philippines by:
GILL & MACMILLAN, LTD.
Goldenbridge, Inchicore
Dublin 8 Ireland

Library of Congress Catalog Card Number: 81-80822
International Standard Book Number
Old Testament Message series: 0-89453-235-9
1-2 Chronicles, Ezra, Nehemiah
0-89453-247-2 (Michael Glazier, Inc.)
7171-1177-6 (Gill & Macmillan, Ltd.)

The Bible text in this publication is from the Revised Standard Version of the
Bible, copyrighted 1946, 1952, ©1971, 1973 by the Division of Christian Education
of the National Council of the Churches of Christ in the U.S.A., and used by
permission.

Cover design by Lillian Brulc

Printed in the United States of America

CONTENTS

FOR MY FATHER AND MOTHER

who first taught me the Word of God

Editors' Preface

Old Testament Message brings into our life and religion today the ancient word of God to Israel. This word, according to the book of the prophet Isaiah, had soaked the earth like "rain and snow coming gently down from heaven" and had returned to God fruitfully in all forms of human life (Isa 55:10). The authors of this series remain true to this ancient Israelite heritage and draw us into the home, the temple and the marketplace of God's chosen people. Although they rely upon the tools of modern scholarship to uncover the distant places and culture of the biblical world, yet they also refocus these insights in a language clear and understandable for any interested reader today. They enable us, even if this be our first acquaintance with the Old Testament, to become sister and brother, or at least good neighbor, to our religious ancestors. In this way we begin to hear God's word ever more forcefully in our own times and across our world, within our prayer and worship, in our secular needs and perplexing problems.

Because life is complex and our world includes, at times in a single large city, vastly different styles of living, we have much to learn from the Israelite Scriptures. The Old Testament spans forty-six biblical books and almost nineteen hundred years of life. It extends through desert, agricultural and urban ways of human existence. The literary style embraces a world of literature and human emotions. Its history began with Moses and the birth-pangs of a new people, it came of age politically and economically under David and Solomon, it reeled under the fiery threats of prophets like Amos and Jeremiah. The people despaired and yet were re-created with new hope during the Babylonian exile. Later reconstruction in the homeland and then the trauma of apocalyptic movements prepared for the revelation of "the mystery hidden for ages in God who created all things" (Eph 3:9).

While the Old Testament telescopes twelve to nineteen hundred years of human existence within the small country of Israel, any single moment of time today witnesses to the reenactment of this entire history across the wide expanse of planet earth. Each verse of the Old Testament is being relived somewhere in our world today. We need, therefore, the *entire* Old Testament and all twenty-three volumes of this new set, in order to be totally a "Bible person" within today's widely diverse society.

The subtitle of this series—"A Biblical-Theological Commentary"—clarifies what these twenty-three volumes intend to do.

Their *purpose* is theological: to feel the pulse of God's word for its *religious* impact and direction.

Their *method* is biblical: to establish the scriptural word firmly within the life and culture of ancient Israel.

Their *style* is commentary: not to explain verse by verse but to follow a presentation of the message that is easily understandable to any serious reader, even if this person is untrained in ancient history and biblical languages.

Old Testament Message—like its predecessor, *New Testament Message*—is aimed at the entire English-speaking world and so is a collaborative effort of an international team. The twenty-one contributors are women and men drawn from North America, Ireland, Britain and Australia. They are scholars who have published in scientific journals, but they have been chosen equally as well for their proven ability to communicate on a popular level. This twenty-three book set comes from Roman Catholic writers, yet, like the Bible itself, it reaches beyond interpretations restricted to an individual church and so enables men and women rooted in biblical faith to unite and so to appreciate their own traditions more fully and more adequately.

Most of all, through the word of God, we seek the blessedness and joy of those

who walk in the law of the Lord!...

who seek God with their whole heart (Ps. 119:1-2).

Carroll Stuhlmueller, C.P.   Martin McNamara, M.S.C.

INTRODUCTION

The books of Chronicles are among the least read books of the Bible. There are articles and books written about the religious ideas of the Old Testament which do not so much as mention them. Very few people would take seriously the warning of St. Jerome: "He who thinks himself acquainted with the sacred writings and does not know these books, only deceives himself." On the surface the books of Chronicles seem to be a mere retelling of the earlier historical material as contained especially in the books of Samuel and Kings and, some would say, a rather dull retelling at that. The purpose in the retelling, however, is to make the message of the past relevant to a new age. Because this has to be undertaken afresh in every age, how it was done already within the Bible itself can have much to say to us today. For this reason the books of Chronicles have an importance all their own within the Bible.

The books of Ezra and Nehemiah are read rather more frequently since they are the main source in the Bible for the understanding of the post-exilic period in the history of Israel. It would be a mistake, however, to think that they present an accurate historical record of the exact way in which the events of that period occurred. The chronology of Ezra and Nehemiah has presented one of the most tantalising riddles of the Bible, the unravelling of which has exercised the minds and imagination of scholars down the years. Too much concern with chronology has obscured somewhat the main function of the books which again, as with

Chronicles, is dealing with reinterpretation — this time of the return from Exile and the restoration of the Temple.

The Socio-Political Background

Jerusalem had fallen to the Babylonians in 587 B.C. and the flower of its people had been taken off into exile in Babylon. With the conquest of Babylon in 539 B.C. by the Persian king, Cyrus, some of their descendants returned to Jerusalem — rather a small number at first — but by 520 B.C. they felt strong enough to set about rebuilding their Temple which had been destroyed by the Babylonians. Early hopes of restoration on a grand scale had not been fulfilled. During the next two hundred years or so, the tiny state around Jerusalem was a mere poverty-stricken backwater of the great Persian Empire, in constant threat of extinction from hostile neighbors without and of dissolution from within by the diminution of its religious ideals. The constant movement of soldiers, statesmen, and merchants passing through on their way to the four corners of the Empire brought an influx of new and alluring ideas and practices.

Theology

It is such a background that forged and hammered out the main ideas of the books of Chronicles, Ezra and Nehemiah. A look at some of these ideas will be a help in understanding the books, especially since many of them betray ways of thinking which are very different to the thought patterns of our own time.

Reinterpretation

There is more than mere updating involved in the Chronicler's rewriting of the past. In Israel there was a very strong belief in the organic unity of the people as a whole, so that past and present together were seen to form one unity which was almost biological in character. The notion of the twelve tribes in Israel could be taken as an example of this. The names of those regarded as the twelve tribes vary from text to text in the Bible but the number *twelve* itself remains constant as a symbol of completeness (cf. 1 Chron 1-9). The Chronicler, in retelling the history, uses twelve as a symbol for the unity of the people as a whole even though by his time only the tribe of Judah in effect was operative.

The word of God spoken in one epoch is just as valid for the next but — and this is the Chronicler's point — in order to be understood it has to be confronted with the new situation and interpreted in its light. This method of procedure is called *Midrash*. The word means a "searching" of Scripture; it is a meditation on the text in order to bring out its meaning for the here and now. Midrash is very often in the form of a sermon and there are many examples of sermons in Chronicles (see below p. 70), inserted at strategic points in the narrative to interpret the text of the older history for the post-exilic period (e.g. 2 Chron 13:4-12; 15:1-7). This of course is what a good sermon is meant to do for the biblical text in our own liturgy. And, just as a good preacher will bring in other Scripture texts to throw light on the one he is trying to interpret, so also the Chronicler very often brings in a collection of biblical passages to make the earlier history relevant for his own time. Thus, for example, in 1 Chron 16 the Chronicler makes use of several psalms to illustrate the relevance of the covenant with David for the people of the post-exilic period.

King and Temple

In the reinterpretation of his people's past, the Chronicler places great emphasis on the foundation of the monarchy in Israel. The books of Chronicles are so structured as to ensure that David and Solomon are regarded as the high point of Israel's history: all that went before is seen as oriented towards them, while that which comes after is patterned on their achievements (see below p. 27ff). In fact the Chronicler largely ignores the earlier foundations of Israel's faith in the Exodus while earlier covenants with Abraham and on Sinai are subsumed into the covenant with David (cf. 1 Chron 16).

By the time of the Chronicler, however, monarchy had disappeared from the land. Why then did he place so much emphasis on it in his retelling of the history? Some writers would see here an evidence of Messianism in the thought of the Chronicler, that is a projection into the future of the hope that was centred in the David of the past. But it seems more likely that the Chronicler's interest was not so much in the monarchy as such but in the plan of God for his people in which David played his own particular role. It is clear from his rewriting of the prophecy of Nathan, for instance, that it is God who is the King for the Chronicler and that the king in Israel was only a medium for establishing God's rule and kingdom (see below p. 47f). Some would see traces of messianic hope also in the way the rebuilding of the Temple is spoken about in Ezra 1-6. But a comparison of this with the books of the post-exilic prophets, Haggai and Zechariah, would indicate rather a playing down of expectations for the restoration of the monarchy (see below p. 162f).

Rather than looking to the future, therefore, it seems fair to say that the Chronicler's hope is solidly based in the post-exilic community gathered around its Temple. God's plan would be worked out in this community if it remained loyal to what had been established through David and Solomon in the past. The David and Solomon portrayed in Chronicles are not the political figures of the earlier histories but the great founders of the Jerusalem Temple and cult. The time of David and Solomon was the time when the foundations were laid for those institutions which in the Chronicler's time were the only source of unity and stability. It is for this reason that an inordinate amount of space within the books is given over to the establishment of the Temple and to its reestablishment after the Exile, since this was the Temple of which the Chronicler had actual experience.

From its completion there was always, in some circles at least, a dissatisfaction with the second Temple (cf. Ezra 3:12).Rabbinic times would later bear witness to this dissatisfaction by saying that five things were lacking in the second Temple which had existed in the first. The five varied but generally included the ark of the covenant, the *Shekinah* (the presence of God) and the Holy Spirit. This dissatisfaction led, in some quarters, to the projection into the future of an ideal Temple and an ideal Jerusalem (cf.Ezek 40-46; Rev 21). The Chronicler shares neither this dissatisfaction nor idealisation. For him the Temple was the one source of stability in a very changing world. It was the life centre of God's people, the privileged place where they met God on earth. There was, then, no interest in finding symbolic meanings for the Temple; it was rather a place of prayer and of worship.

The Levites

The Levites as the cult personnel of the Temple are given great prominence in the books. They played an important role in the preservation of religious practices in the post-exilic period. The origins of the Levites are shrouded in the mists of antiquity. In the Bible, they appear as the descendants of Levi, one of the twelve sons of Israel, and are presented as set apart by God to perform the functions of the cult. They functioned in a priestly role at various sanctuaries in Israel's early history (cf. Judg 17:10) and were also responsible for teaching the law of Moses to the people (Deut 33:10). One line among them was gradually alone considered for the priesthood, especially at the central sanctuary in Jerusalem (see below p. 60), while the remainder of the Levites assumed a subordinate role in the cult or were scattered throughout the land (Deut 12:12; cf. Ezek 40:46).

The Chronicler's picture of the Levites takes account of their increased importance in the Jerusalem of post-exilic times. Their tasks were greatly expanded to include musical and security functions in the cult (e.g. 1 Chron 25-26) and administrative and teaching posts among the people (e.g. 1

Chron 9:26; Neh 8:7, 9). Throughout the books the main vehicle for conveying the Chronicler's theology was what has come to be called the "levitical sermon." In fact it is possible to tell the importance of an historical event for the Chronicler quite often by the presence or absence of such sermons (see below p. 70).

What is most characteristic of the Chronicler's point of view, however, is the way in which he chooses to identify the Levites of his own time with the prophets of Israel's past, and, in accordance with his usual custom, he projects backwards this identification, making singers of the monarchic period also into prophets (see below p. 62). He sees the essential duty of the singers, the cultic song, as a prophetic performance (cf. 1 Chron 25:2). Prophetic traditions on the whole were of great importance to the Chronicler. It was by prophecy that the monarchy was founded (1 Chron 11:3), reproved (e.g. 2 Chron 24:20) and finally destroyed (2 Chron 36:15-16). The post-exilic activities of the prophets Haggai and Zechariah are all important for the Chronicler but he puts his own interpretation on their message; confining himself to their intervention on behalf of the restoration of the Temple (Ezra 5-6) and ignoring their interest in the restoration of the monarchy (see below p. 162).

The word of God could be mediated not only through traditional prophets but also through the inspired musician of the Temple liturgy (e.g. 2 Chron 29:25) or the king (e.g. 2 Chron 13:4-12). Such "prophecies" are more in the nature of commentaries on earlier texts of the Bible than actual new insights (e.g. 2 Chron 15:2-7). This is again an example of the kind of updating that was going on all the time within these books (see p. 2). As in the Deuteronomistic tradition, genuine trust in God and devout prayer is seen as a necessary prerequisite for keeping the Law of God in response to the prophetic word (e.g. 1 Chron 28:9,10; cf. Deut 4:29). The law which is often mentioned in Chronicles can be the unified expression of God's will in the written Torah (e.g. 2 Chron 35:26) but it can also be the keeping of the diversified laws of ritual connected with the Temple (e.g. 1 Chron

16:40). The Chronicler's use of these laws indicates that he was acquainted with the Priestly writing which is part of the Pentateuch as we know it.

"All Israel"

The unity of the people envisioned by the Chronicler is not only sociological; it is above all a unity in faith. A favourite phrase of the Chronicler for this unity is "all Israel." For him the covenants of the past between God and his people were made with all twelve tribes (1 Chron 16:14-16). These covenants had been renewed in David (2 Chron 13:4-5) and the Chronicler is careful to portray David as gathering the whole people for all the major events of his reign (e.g. 1 Chron 11:1; 12:23-40). The Chronicler therefore viewed the subsequent split of the Kingdom into North and South as a sundering of God's people (2 Chron 13:4-12). The North is ignored as a political entity but there is a constant call to its people to join again in the unity which finds its centre in the Jerusalem cult (e.g. 2 Chron 30:1).

For the beleaguered Jerusalem community of his own time the message is two-pronged: on the one hand there is the realisation that the same God who had spoken to their ancestors in the past now speaks to them as well. Their God is still the Judge of the world; even if his people seem threatened by great and powerful nations they are not to fear because God is on their side just as he was in the past (e.g. 2 Chron 20:1-30). On the other hand there is a warning against exclusivism which was a very real danger to the post-exilic community. The Chronicler amply demonstrates from the history of the monarchy that a faithful remnant must not exclude others (e.g. 2 Chron 30:1). Rather than appearing as a ghetto, Jerusalem should prove a magnet drawing together the people who had been scattered far and wide by dispersion, by exile and by schism (e.g. 2 Chron 15:9; Ezra 1:3).

Retribution

The books of Chronicles contain the most consistent

teaching in the Bible on the theology of individual retribution, that is the concept that fidelity to God is rewarded while infidelity is punished — in this life, of course, because the idea of retribution in the next life had not yet occurred to the people of the time. For the Chronicler, punishment followed sin with unerring stroke but at the same time repentance was always possible and this could reverse the punishment or at least modify it (see below p. 27 and p. 136).

It is chiefly to the individual kings in Israel that this theory is rigorously applied; blessings or misfortune come to the people as a whole because of the action of the king. So, for example, faithfulness on the part of the king resulted in peace and prosperity for the people (e.g. 2 Chron 20:30) and numerous offspring and success for the king himself (e.g. 2 Chron 13:19-21). On the other hand, infidelity led to defeat and conquest (e.g. 2 Chron 12:5) and also sickness and disease, from plague (1 Chron 21:1-14) and leprosy (2 Chron 26:16-21) to sore feet (2 Chron 16:12).

The Chronicler's stress on individual retribution differs from the more collective idea of retribution evident in his sources in Samuel-Kings. So, for example, in allocating blame for the eventual fall of Jerusalem to the Babylonians, the Chronicler insists that since guilt cannot be held over from one reign to the next, the last king of Judah, Zedekiah, and his nobles must take full responsibility for the debacle (2 Chron 36:11-21). In Kings, on the other hand, it is the accumulated guilt of earlier reigns which is responsible for the downfall of the state (2 Kings 24:1-4; 18-20 see below p. 144).

One can be dismayed by the narrowness of the Chronicler on the question of retribution but what has to be remembered is that it was only one insight in the progressive understanding of God and of his relations with his people. If the Chronicler had not put his doctrine of individual retribution so starkly and rigidly, perhaps such a work as the book of Job might never have been written with its almost wild reaction to the neat orthodoxy of retribution.

Author and Date

Most scholars would see the late Persian period (400-333 B.C., see p. 2) as a significant time in the composition of Chronicles and Ezra-Nehemiah, but there is a wide variety of opinion as to whether this was the final stage of composition or the period in which the bulk of the work was completed allowing for later additions and accretions. Again there is difference of opinion as to whether the author who composed Chronicles also wrote Ezra and Nehemiah. The belief in common authorship was based on the supposed similarity between the books in style, choice of vocabulary, outlook and theology. Recent exhaustive research, however, has pointed out the great divergence that is also there, so much so that many would suggest that Chronicles is a completely separate work from Ezra-Nehemiah. Others would continue to keep the unity of the books and would stress instead various editions of Chronicles and Ezra-Nehemiah. Theories differ as to the extent of these additions (see below p. 147).

There is no doubt that the final work as we now have it does bear signs of additions and accretions but there is also distinct evidence of deliberate overall organisation of the material. For example, the books of Ezra and Nehemiah seem to be deliberately paralleled one with the other and both echo preoccupations of Chronicles especially in relation to the Temple (see below p. 147f). The first nine chapters of 1 Chronicles which are often considered as an addition to the book, also bear a very strong relationship to the material of the remainder of the books of Chronicles (see below p. 11). The stages of the composition of the books will no doubt exercise the minds and imagination of scholars for many a decade. For the purposes of this commentary, however, the blanket term, *the Chronicler*, will continue to be used for the author(s) of the books, the more obvious signs of different authorship being pointed out as they occur.

1 and 2 Chronicles

The books of Chronicles can be divided into four main sections:

I. Family Trees (1 Chron 1:1—9:34)

II. David Founder of the Temple Cult (1 Chron 9:35—29:30)

III. Solomon Builder of the Temple (2 Chron 1:1—9:31)

IV. Good and Bad Kings in Judah (2 Chron 10:1—36:23).

The first section of Chronicles (1 Chron 1-9) is made up of unexciting lists of names. At first glance these seem to be a collection of all the genealogical tables of earlier books of the Bible but closer inspection reveals that there is definite purpose and organisation in the arrangement of these genealogical tables. Some scholars would suggest that they did not form part of the original work of the Chronicler but that, even though it is possible that lists were added onto here and there, their overall preoccupations as we have them now are closely linked with the main concerns of the books of Chronicles as a whole. Their purpose is to give a solid foundation to the emergence of the kingdom of David and Solomon and of the Temple cult which they founded (see Introduction p. 3).

In the genealogies, therefore, the emergence of David in Israel is set against the larger background of Israel as a nation (1 Chron 1) and of the twelve tribes among which the tribe of David, Judah, is given prominence (1 Chron 2-8). The importance of the Temple and of its cult personnel in the main body of Chronicles finds its counterpoint in 1 Chron 1-9 with a detailed genealogy of the Levites (1 Chron

6), while the all-pervasive theme of Chronicles, that of present stability based on past foundations, is echoed in the list of returned exiles at the end of the genealogies (1 Chron 9). This provides a bridge between past and present.

I. FAMILY TREES
1 Chron 1:1—9:34.

An interest in family records is a characteristic of our times. People travelling to the country of their origins take great pains to trace their ancestors as far back as they can go. Finding one's roots gives a great sense of stability and continuity. This is especially true in periods of disillusionment and of disruption. The long lists of names in the first nine chapters of Chronicles show the same interest in the past; they come from a period in Israel's history when the need for stability and continuity was strongly felt. Firmly anchored in the past, it would be possible to face the future with confidence.

The Chronicler's use of genealogies and other lists is really a work of art. Instead of relying on poetry or narrative to get his message across he uses what could, in ordinary circumstances, be very dead material indeed. Perhaps his art is not as far-fetched as one might think when one considers the skill with which statistics are used today. It is amazing how often the same "objective" lists can be pressed into service to support opposing economic or political stances.

It will not be possible, nor even necessary, to quote all the nine chapters of genealogical tables in 1 Chronicles 1-9. Certain passages are chosen below to give the flavour of the whole.

THE EMERGENCE OF ISRAEL
1:1-54.

1 Adam, Seth, Enosh; ²Kenan, Mahalalel, Jared; ³Enoch, Methuselah, Lamech; ⁴Noah, Shem, Ham, and Japheth.

⁵The sons of Japheth: Gomer, Magog, Madai, Javan, Tubal, Meshech, and Tiras. ⁶The sons of Gomer: Ashkenaz, Diphath, and Togarmah. ⁷The sons of Javan: Elishah, Tarshish, Kittim, and Rodanim.

⁸The sons of Ham: Cush, Egypt, Put, and Canaan. ⁹The sons of Cush: Seba, Havilah, Sabta, Raama, and Sabteca. The sons of Raamah: Sheba and Dedan. ¹⁰Cush was the father of Nimrod; he began to be a mighty one in the earth.

¹¹Egypt was the father of Ludim, Anamim, Lehabim, Naphtuhim, ¹²Pathrusim, Casluhim (whence came the Philistines), and Caphtorim.

¹³Canaan was the father of Sidon his first-born, and Heth, ¹⁴and the Jebusites, the Amorites, the Girgashites, ¹⁵the Hivites, the Arkites, the Sinites, ¹⁶the Arvadites, the Zemarites, and the Hamathites.

¹⁷The sons of Shem: Elam, Asshur, Arpachshad, Lud, Aram, Uz, Hul, Gether, and Meshech. ¹⁸Arpachshad was the father of Shelah; and Shelah was the father of Eber. ¹⁹To Eber were born two sons: the name of the one was Peleg (for in his days the earth was divided), and the name of his brother Joktan. ²⁰Joktan was the father of Almodad, Sheleph, Hazarmaveth, Jerah, ²¹Hadoram, Uzal, Diklah, ²²Ebal, Abimael, Sheba, ²³Ophir, Havilah, and Jobab; all these were the sons of Joktan.

²⁴Shem, Arpachshad, Shelah; ²⁵Eber, Peleg, Reu; ²⁶Serug, Nahor, Terah; ²⁷Abram, that is, Abraham.

²⁸The sons of Abraham: Isaac and Ishmael. ²⁹These are their genealogies: the first-born of Ishmael, Nebaioth; and Kedar, Adbeel, Mibsam, ³⁰Mishma, Dumah, Massa, Hadad, Tema, ³¹Jetur, Naphish, and Kedemah. These

are the sons of Ishmael. ³²The sons of Keturah, Abra-
ham's concubine: she bore Zimran, Jokshan, Medan,
Midian, Ishbak, and Shuah. The sons of Jokshan: Sheba
and Dedan. ³³The sons of Midian: Ephah, Epher,
Hanoch, Abida, and Eldaah. All these were the de-
scendants of Keturah.
    ³⁴Abraham was the father of Isaac.The sons of Isaac:
Esau and Israel. ³⁵The sons of Esau: Eliphaz, Reuel,
Jeush, Jalam, and Korah. ³⁶The sons of Eliphaz: Teman,
Omar, Zephi, Gatam, Kenaz, Timna, and Amalek. ³⁷The
sons of Reuel: Nahath, Zerah, Shammah, and Mizzah.

The Chronicler's way of retelling the early history of his
people, then, is to present us with a summary list of names.
These genealogies are not always strictly biological in make-
up. Often historical continuity is presented as physical descent. It is quite obvious that some names appearing as
ancestors are really place or clan names. For example the
countries, Egypt and Canaan, are mentioned as sons of
Ham in 1:8. "Son of" in Semitic terminology can stand for a
much wider relationship than mere descent. So there is the
case, for instance, of the prophet Samuel being considered a
"son of" Levi (cf. 6:16-30) even though he belonged to
another tribe altogether (cf. 1 Sam 1:1). He is reckoned a
Levite because of his relationship to the sanctuary.
    In chapter one, the Chronicler situates Israel in the wider
context of humanity as a whole. Beginning with Adam, he
eliminates all the lines of world peoples which do not lead to
Israel before eventually coming to its own history. Situating
Israel within humanity as a whole is deliberate, highlighting
God's choice and his sovereignty over all mankind.
    The Chronicler shows no interest in the call of Abraham
nor in God's covenant with him as he would later ignore the
Exodus and the covenant with Moses on Sinai (see Intro. p.
3). Such founding events of the people's history are subsumed into the founding of the Temple and the covenant
with David. It is necessary to stress this lack of interest in the
Exodus in particular since much recent writing on the Bible

tends to treat the Exodus as the core experience of the
people of Israel and to see all later events in their history as
modelled on that experience of liberation. The Chronicler's
history within the Bible is one large section of the literature
which bypasses this tradition. Indeed, if we only had his way
of presenting the past we would be justified in questioning
whether there ever was an Exodus at all. For him the land
itself was all important and the unity of the people within
that land was to be fostered at all costs (see Intro. p. 7).

THE BACKGROUND TO DAVID
2:1—3:24.

2 These are the sons of Israel: Reuben, Simeon, Levi,
Judah, Issachar, Zebulun, [2]Dan, Joseph, Benjamin,
Naphtali, Gad, and Asher. [3]The sons of Judah: Er, Onan,
and Shelah; these three Bathshua the Canaanitess bore
to him. Now Er, Judah's first-born, was wicked in the
sight of the Lord, and he slew him. [4]His daughter-in-law
Tamar also bore him Perez and Zerah. Judah had five
sons in all.
[5]The sons of Perez: Hezron and Hamul....
[9]The sons of Hezron, that were born to him: Jerahmeel,
Ram, and Chelubai. [10]Ram was the father of Amminadab, and Amminadab was the father of Nahshon,
prince of the sons of Judah. [11]Nahshon was the father
of Salma, Salma of Boaz, [12]Boaz of Obed, Obed of Jesse.
[13]Jesse was the father of Eliab his first-born, Abinadab
the second, Shimea the third, [14]Nethanel the fourth,
Raddai the fifth, [15]Ozem the sixth, David the seventh;
[16]and their sisters were Zeruiah and Abigail. The sons
of Zeruiah: Abishai, Joab, and Asahel, three. [17]Abigail
bore Amasa, and the father of Amasa was Jether the
Ishmaelite....
3 These are the sons of David that were born to him
in Hebron: the first-born Amnon, by Ahinoam the Jezre-
elitess; the second Daniel, by Abigail the Carmelitess,

²the third Absalom, whose mother was Maacah, the daughter of Talmai, king of Geshur; the fourth Adonijah, whose mother was a Haggith; ³the fifth Shephatiah, by Abital; the sixth Ithream, by his wife Eglah; ⁴six were born to him in Hebron, where he reigned for seven years and six months. And he reigned thirty-three years in Jerusalem. ⁵These were born to him in Jerusalem: Shimea, Shobab, Nathan, and Solomon, four by Bathshua, the daughter of Ammiel; ⁶then Ibhar, Elishama, Eliphelet. ⁷Nogah, Nepheg, Japhia, ⁸Elishama, Eliada, and Eliphelet, nine. ⁹All these were David's sons, besides the sons of the concubines; and Tamar was their sister.

¹⁰The descendants of Solomon: Rehoboam, Abijah his son, Asa his son, Jehoshaphat his son, ¹¹Joram his son, Ahaziah his son, Joash his son, ¹²Amaziah his son, Azariah his son, Jotham his son, ¹³Ahaz his son, Hezekiah his son, Manasseh his son, ¹⁴Amon his son, Josiah his son. ¹⁵The sons of Josiah: Johanan the first-born, the second Jehoiakim, the third Zedekiah, the fourth Shallum. ¹⁶The descendants of Jehoiakim: Jeconiah his son, Zedekiah his son; ¹⁷and the sons of Jeconiah, the captive: Shealtiel his son, ¹⁸Malchiram, Pedaiah, Shenazzar, Jekamiah, Hoshama, and Nedabiah; ¹⁹and the sons of Pedaiah: Zerubbabel and Shimei; and the sons of Zerubbabel: Meshullam and Hananiah, and Shelomith was their sister; ²⁰and Hashubah, Ohel, Berechiah, Hasadiah, and Jushabhesed, five. ²¹The sons of Hananiah: Pelatiah and Jeshaiah, his son Rephaiah, his son Arnan, his son Obadiah, his son Shecaniah. ²²The sons of Shecaniah: Shemaiah. And the sons of Shemaiah: Hattush, Igal, Bariah, Neariah, and Shaphat, six. ²³The sons of Neariah: Elioenai, Hizkiah, and Azrikam, three. ²⁴The sons of Elioenai: Hodaviah, Eliashib, Pelaiah, Akkub, Johanan, Delaiah, and Anani, seven.

The descendants of the twelve tribes are listed in the following chapters. The aim seems to be to give as broad a base as possible to the emergence of the kingdom of David;

the tribe of Judah from which David came is treated first in chapter two while the genealogies of David are given in detail in chapter three. The sons born to him at Jerusalem are listed elsewhere in Chronicles (cf. 1 Chron 14:3-7); not so those born in Hebron (cf. 2 Sam 3:2-5). The descendants of David listed in vv.10-16 comprise the Davidic dynasty in Judah down to the Exile as outlined in the books of Kings —with the exception of the queen Athaliah (cf. 2 Chron 22:10-23:15).

The post-exilic line of David is traced through Jeconiah (Jehoiachin) who is given the title "the captive." According to Chronicles (cf. 2 Chron 36:3-10) he was the second king to be taken captive to Babylon his father, Jehoiakim, having preceeded him there. Kings is probably more accurate in suggesting that Jehoiakim died in Jerusalem (cf. 2 Kings 24:6) and also in saying that Jeconiah was eighteen years old when he began to reign rather than the "eight" years of Chronicles (cf. 2 Kings 24:8; 2 Chron 36:9). Five of Jeconiah's sons mentioned in the genealogy are also mentioned in contemporary documents as receiving rations from the Babylonian authorities. One of them, Shenazzar, has often been equated with the leader of the returned exiles, Sheshbazzar, (cf. Ezra 1:8; 5:14-16). It would surely have been at least mentioned if Sheshbazzar were of Davidic descent since this is stressed for the leader who came after him, Zerubbabel (cf. Ezra 3:2) who was a grandson of Jeconiah. Zerubbabel's father's name is given in the genealogy as Pedaiah, but as Shealtiel in Ezra. Perhaps Shealtiel died childless and, according to Levirite family law (cf. Mt 22:23-33), Pedaiah would have married his widow. The resulting son would be legally a son of Shealtiel.

The geneology of Jeconiah carries on for six generations. It is difficult to say whether the presence of this list indicates an interest in Messianism on the part of the Chronicler (see Intro. p. 4) or whether it merely indicates a large number of Davidites among the post-exilic community who were interested in preserving their ancestry. As it is placed, here it seems to act as a visible link between the post-exilic situation and the past glory of the monarchy and so would bear witness to the deliberate linking of the geneologies to the content of the book as a whole (see p. 1).

OTHER TRIBES
4:1—5:26; 7:1—8:40.

7 [20]The sons of Ephraim: Shuthelah, and Bered his son, Tahath his son, Eleadah his son, Tahath his son, [21]Zabad his son, Shuthelah his son, and Ezer and Elead, whom the men of Gath who were born in the land slew, because they came down to raid their cattle. [22]And Ephraim their father mourned many days, and his brothers came to comfort him. [23]And Ephraim went in to his wife, and she conceived and bore a son; and he called his name Beriah, because evil had befallen his house. [24]His daughter was Sheerah, who built both Lower and Upper Bethhoron, and Uzzensheerah. [25]Rephah was his son, Resheph his son, Telah his son, Tahan his son, [26]Ladan his son, Ammihud his son, Elishama his son, [27]Nun his son, Joshua his son. [28]Their possessions and settlements were Bethel and its towns, and eastward Naaran, and westward Gezer and its towns, Shechem and its towns, and Ayyah and its towns; [29]also along the borders of the Manassites, Bethshean and its towns, Taanach and its towns, Megiddo and its towns, Dor and its towns. In these dwelt the sons of Joseph the son of Israel.

The remainder of the tribe of Judah is listed in chapter four; the other tribes are then accounted for. Three different types of material have been isolated in these genealogies:
a) core material: the actual genealogy itself (e.g. 7:20-21a; 25-27);
b) geographical data: details of settlements and possessions (e.g. 7:24; 28-29);
c) miscellaneous data: odd bits of historical information

which shed light on individuals or tribes. For example, in chapter seven above, information is given about the death of Ephraim's sons through a cattle raid and the naming of a further son is said to relate to that incident. (7:21b-23).

The question has often been asked why such material should find its way into genealogies but recent discoveries of Bedouin genealogies from the Syrian desert reveal the presence of similar details as a prominent feature of lists of ancestors. The insertion can include information about tribal warfare, unusual events or places of temporary settlement. The following example is not unlike what is to be found in 7:21b: "By Garam- 'el b. Dhi'b b. Kaun. And the torrent drove him away at the watering place of camels in the year in which the tribe of Kadam drove away the tribe of Harim.   So, O Allāt, give peace!" (see other interesting examples and sources in, H. G. W. Williamson, *Israel in the Books of Chronicles,* pp. 76-79).

THE LEVITES
6:1-81.

6 The sons of Levi: Gershom, Kohath, and Merari. [2]The sons of Kohath: Amram, Izhar, Hebron, and Uzziel. [3]The children of Amram: Aaron, Moses, and Miriam. The sons of Aaron: Nadab, Abihu, Eleazar, and Ithamar. [4]Eleazar was the father of Phinehas of Abishua, [5]Abishua of Bukki, Bukki of Uzzi, [6]Uzzi of Zerahiah, Zerahiah of Meraioth, [7]Meraioth of Amariah, Amariah of Ahitub, [8]Ahitub of Zadok, Zadok of Ahimaaz, [9]Ahimaaz of Azariah, Azariah of Johanan, [10]and Johanan of Azariah (it was he who served as priest in the house that Solomon built in Jerusalem). [11]Azariah was the father of Amariah, Amariah of Ahitub, [12]Ahitub of Zadok, Zadok of Shallum, [13]Shallum of Hilkiah, Hilkiah of Azariah, [14]Azariah of Seraiah, Seraiah of Jehozadak; [15]and Jehozadak went into exile when the Lord sent Judah and Jerusalem into exile by the hand of Nebuchadnezzar.

¹⁶The sons of Levi: Gershom, Kohath, and Merari. ¹⁷And these are the names of the sons of Gershom: Libni and Shimei. ¹⁸The sons of Kohath: Amram, Izhar, Hebron, and Uzziel. ¹⁹The sons of Merari: Mahli and Mushi. These are the families of the Levites according to their fathers. ²⁰Of Gershom: Libni his son, Jahath his son, Zimmah his son, ²¹Joah his son, Iddo his son, Zerah his son, Jeatherai his son. ²²The sons of Kohath: Amminadab his son, Korah his son, Assir his son, ²³Elkanah his son, Ebiasaph his son, Assir his son, ²⁴Tahath his son, Uriel his son, Uzziah his son, and Shaul his son. ²⁵The sons of Elkanah: Amasai and Ahimoth, ²⁶Elkanah his son, Zophai his son, Nahath his son, ²⁷Eliab his son, Jeroham his son, Elkanah his son. ²⁸The sons of Samuel: Joel his first-born, the second Abijah. ²⁹The sons of Merari: Mahli, Libni his son, Shimei his son, Uzzah his son, ³⁰Shimea his son, Haggiah his son, and Asaiah his son.

³¹These are the men whom David put in charge of the service of song in the house of the Lord, after the ark rested there. ³²They ministered with song before the tabernacle of the tent of meeting, until Solomon had built the house of the Lord in Jerusalem; and they performed their service in due order. ³³These are the men who served and their sons. Of the sons of the Kohathites: Heman the singer the son of Joel, son of Samuel, ³⁴son of Elkanah, son of Jeroham, son of Eliel, son of Toah, ³⁵son of Zuph, son of Elkanah, son of Mahath, son of Amasai, ³⁶son of Elkanah, son of Joel, son of Azariah, son of Zephaniah, ³⁷son of Tahath, son of Assir, son of Ebiasaph, son of Korah, ³⁸son of Izhar, son of Kohath, son of Levi, son of Israel; ³⁹and his brother Asaph, who stood on his right hand, namely, Asaph the son of Berechiah, son of Shimea, ⁴⁰son of Michael, son of Baaseiah, son of Malchijah, ⁴¹son of Ethni, son of Zerah, son of Adaiah, ⁴²son of Ethan, son of Zimmah, son of Shimei,

⁴³son of Jahath, son of Gershom, son of Levi. ⁴⁴On the left hand were their brethren the sons of Merari: Ethan the son of Kishi, son of Abdi, son of Malluch, ⁴⁵son of Hashabiah,...

⁵⁴These are their dwelling places according to their settlements within their borders: to the sons of Aaron of the families of Kohathites, for theirs was the lot, ⁵⁵to them they gave Hebron in the land of Judah and its surrounding pasture lands, ⁵⁶but the fields of the city and its villages they gave to Caleb the son of Jephunneh. ⁵⁷To the sons of Aaron theygave the cities of refuge: Hebron, Libnah with its pasture lands, Jattir, Eshtemoa with its pasture lands, ⁵⁸Hilen with its pasture lands, Debir with its pasture lands, ⁵⁹Ashan with its pasture lands, and Bethshemesh with its pasture lands; ⁶⁰and from the tribe of Benjamin, Geba with its pasture lands, Alemeth with its pasture lands, and Anathoth with its pasture lands. All their cities throughout their families were thirteen.

Among the genealogies of the tribes, that of the Levites is given special attention because of their special function in the Temple cult (see Intro. p. 5). The opening section of the chapter gives the descendents of Levi through his three sons: Gershom, Kohath and Merari. The line then followed is that through Kohath alone from whom Aaron was descended (the other branches are taken up again in vv. 16-30). Aaron's line is followed in some detail especially as it proceeded through his son, Eleazar. The purpose of this seems to be to give the main priestly line down to the Exile (vv.4-15). This is complemented in Neh 12:10-11 by a list of the chief priests after the Exile (see p. 147). Continuity with the past was the all important emphasis in these lists (see p. 1) but an emphasis on legitimacy of ancestry (real or contrived) is also important in the genealogy of the Levites. Legitimacy was a necessary precondition for having a function in the post-exilic cult (cf. Ezra 2:62-63; Neh 7:64-65).

One of the chief functions of the Levites for the Chronicler was that of singers in the cult (see Intro. p. 6). In this chapter they are authenticated as such in two directions: firstly, by the insistence that they were appointed to that office by David who was regarded as the founder of liturgical music (cf. 1 Chron 25); secondly, by tracing their genealogies back to the three sons of Levi. Continuity and legitimacy are again closely linked by this arrangement. The three most famous musicians of Israel's history: Asaph, Heman and Ethan (or Jeduthun cf. 1 Chron 25:1), are included in the levitical genealogies. Only the family of Asaph is mentioned in the post-exilic lists as returning from Exile (cf. Ezra 2:41; Neh 7:44). The other two are reported elsewhere in 1 Chronicles as belonging to the sanctuary of Gibeon (1 Chron 16:37; 41).

Also listed in this chapter are the levitical cities, said to have been given to the Levites on coming into the land as a substitute for the tracts of land which the other tribes received (cf. Josh 21). The passage is typical of the way the Chronicler uses material from Joshua and Judges to substantiate the post-exilic claim to the land; many of the cities mentioned in the list are considered Canaanite possessions in Judg 1:29-36 but, for the Chronicler, they were securely in the hands of the Levites from the beginning (cf. 1 Chron 13:1-5). Attachment to the land was an important element of his theology. What the distribution of the Levites in cities also underlines is that they formed a distinct group in Israel, not because they lived in one region but because they all performed the same function in society wherever they were.

PAST INTO PRESENT
9:1-34.

9 So all Israel was enrolled by genealogies; and these are written in the Book of the Kings of Israel. And Judah was taken into exile in Babylon because of their unfaithfulness. ²Now the first to dwell again in their possessions in their cities were Israel, the priests, the Levites, and the temple servants. ³And some of the people of Judah,

Benjamin, Ephraim, and Manasseh dwelt in Jerusalem: [4]Uthai the son of Ammihud, son of Omri, son of Imri, son of Bani, from the sons of Perez the son of Judah. [5]And of the Shilonites: Asaiah the first-born, and his sons. [6]Of the sons of Zerah: Jeuel and their kinsmen, six hundred and ninety. [7]Of the Benjaminites: Sallu the son of Meshullam, son of Hodaviah, son of Hassenuah, [8]Ibneiah the son of Jeroham, Elah the son of Uzzi, son of Michri, and Meshullam the son of Shephatiah, son of Reuel, son of Ibnijah; [9]and their kinsmen according to their generations, nine hundred and fifty-six. All these were heads of fathers' houses according to their fathers' houses.

The essential link between the past and the time of the Chronicler is forged in chapter nine. It gives supposed lists of those who returned after the Exile and so bridges the gap caused by the collapse of the nation at the fall of Jerusalem (cf. Ezra 2; Neh 7, 11). The lesson is driven home by the Chronicler that the people who might have seemed so hopeless and lost, scattered as they were in the midst of powerful nations, could again hold its head high. Israel has had a glorious past, a past which is far from dead. By means of these lists, the Chronicler ensures the march of the past into the present in order to give hope and light to those who are dispirited.

Four classes of returning exiles are mentioned: the laity, priests, Levites and temple slaves. Among the laity the mention of "Judah, Benjamin, Ephraim and Manasseh" stresses the fact that "all Israel" is included in the return (see Intro. p. 7); Judah and Benjamin comprise the South while Ephraim and Manasseh stood for the North as its most important tribes (cf. 2 Chron 30).

Much of this list will appear again in Neh 11 but there it will serve as a list of family heads who lived in Judah in the time of Nehemiah (see p. 207). It is probable that a census list is at the back of both chapters, or perhaps two forms of the same list, since there are many similarities between them.

One interesting difference is the lack of any mention of Ephraim and Manasseh in Nehemiah 11. This may indicate a more exclusive attitude in the book of Nehemiah (see p. 207).

II. DAVID, FOUNDER OF THE TEMPLE CULT
1 Chron 9:35-29:30

SAUL: THE PREDECESSOR OF DAVID
9:35-10:13

[35]In Gibeon dwelt the father of Gibeon, Jeiel, and the name of his wife was Maacah, [36]and his first-born son Abdon, then Zur, Kish, Baal, Ner, Nadab, [37]Gedor, Ahio, Zechariah, and Mikloth; [38]and Mikloth was the father of Shimeam; and these also dwelt opposite their kinsmen in Jerusalem, with their kinsmen. [39]Ner was the father of Kish, Kish of Saul, Saul of Jonathan. . . .
10 Now the Philistines fought against Israel; and the men of Israel fled before the Philistines, and fell slain on Mount Gilboa. [2]And the Philistines overtook Saul and his sons; and the Philistines slew Jonathan and Abinadab and Malchishua, the sons of Saul. . . .

[13]So Saul died for his unfaithfulness; he was unfaithful to the Lord in that he did not keep the command of the Lord, and also consulted a medium, seeking guidance, [14]and did not seek guidance from the Lord. Therefore the Lord slew him, and turned the kingdom over to David the son of Jesse.

At the end of chapter nine the genealogy of Saul is repeated. This marks the transition from the genealogies to the narrative section of the book. The remainder of 1 Chronicles will treat of David but first of all his right to the kingship has to be authenticated. This is achieved by showing where the first king of Israel went wrong and by treating his line as abruptly cut short. It is easy to see that the Chronicler's account of the story of Saul is only told as a foil to the story of David even though none of the details from the earlier historical books of the interaction between David and Saul are related. Only the bare bones of Saul's story are given. The story as such would have been too well-known to need recounting in detail.

There is none of the poignancy, then, of the earlier account of Saul's life: a man who had great potential but who failed so tragically. The account in 1 Samuel hints that the reason for his failure lay in some personality defect and shows a certain sympathy for him. This sympathy is not shared by the Chronicler. For him there is only one verdict: Saul sinned, therefore he was punished. His crime was that he did not keep the word of God (1 Sam 13:8-15; 15:1-33) and he consulted the witch of Endor (1 Sam 28:7-19). This judgment is the first example of the Chronicler's theory of individual retribution (see Intro. p. 8) and will be typical of his reaction to sinfulness in later kings (cf. 2 Chron 12:2; 21:10; 25:20). It is possible that for him, Saul was a paradigm of what a king should not be, whereas David was very much the pattern of the ideal king.

The message for his own generation lay not with Saul but with David, so the Chronicler quickly turns the pages of history to reach his hero.

THE KINGSHIP OF DAVID
11:1-14:17.

The remainder of 1 Chronicles will have David at the centre of the stage. Let us take a look first of all at the implications of the Chronicler's portrait of David before going into details of the king's activities. As stated in the

Introduction (p. 3f), the Chronicler was representing the history of his people according to the preoccupations of his own time and this is nowhere more evident than in his treatment of David. The David of the earlier historical books (1 and 2 Samuel) could be characterised as a Robin Hood type of outlaw who by means of the power of his personality and intrigue managed to work his way into the kingship after the convenient death of Saul. The Chronicler's portrait is the exact opposite: a good pious king concerned above all with the worship of his God. Which is the real David?

The historical truth probably lies somewhere in between these two points of view. Literary critics today would question whether the account in the Books of Samuel is as totally biographical as has been generally assumed. They would see much legendary material even, for example, in the colourful story of David's affair with Bathsheba. The historical David was probably both saint and sinner but always with a genuine devotion to Yahweh his God and dependence on him. It is this latter aspect which appealed to the Chronicler and he concentrates on it to the almost total exclusion of the older and, to our way of thinking, the more human account. We should see the two portraits of David as complementary rather than as contradictory.

David Unites the People
11:1-3

11 Then all Israel gathered together to David at Hebron, and said "Behold, we are your bone and flesh. [2]In times past, even when Saul was king, it was you that led out and brought in Israel; and the Lord your God said to you, 'You shall be shepherd of my people Israel, and you shall be prince over my people Israel.' " [3]So all the elders of Israel came to the king at Hebron; and David made a covenant with them at Hebron before the Lord, and they anointed David king over Israel, according to the word of the Lord by Samuel.

The fact that the Chronicler does indeed presume his reader's knowledge of the earlier historical books is abundantly clear throughout the text of 1 Chronicles. He starts his treatment of David's reign with an account of his kingship in Hebron omitting all that led up to this. David was first of all appointed king of Hebron by his fellow tribesmen from Judah (cf. 2 Sam 2:4). The Chronicler omits this in favour of the incident some time after the death of Saul when the remainder of the tribes finally came over to him (2 Sam 5). The telescoping of the two events makes the Chronicler's point that all twelve tribes are necessary to the fullness of the people of Israel and so must be seen to be present right from the beginning of the ideal monarchy (see Intro. p. 3). The unity of Israel and the sovereignty of David are thus complementary.

The beautiful image of the king as shepherd of his people is preserved from 2 Samuel (cf. 5:2). It was an image that was especially suitable to David, given his background, and it was one that would be frequently used for kingship in the other books of the Bible (e.g. Ezek 34:23-24; 37:24-25; Ps 78 [77]:70-72; cf. Jn 10). David's appointment as king is seen as not coming from human power but is "according to the word of the Lord by Samuel" (cf. 1 Sam 16).

Capture of Jerusalem
11:4-9

⁴And David and all Israel went to Jerusalem, that is Jebus, where the Jebusites were, the inhabitants of the land. ⁵The inhabitants of Jebus said to David, "You will not come in here." Nevertheless David took the stronghold of Zion, that is, the city of David. ⁶David said, "Whoever shall smite the Jebusites first shall be chief and commander." And Joab the son of Zeruiah went up first, so he became chief. ⁷And David dwelt in the stronghold; therefore it was called the city of David. ⁸And he built the city round about from the Millo in complete circuit; and Joab repaired the rest of the city. ⁹And David became greater and greater, for the Lord of hosts was with him.

"All Israel" has now got a king; with the capture of Jerusalem it also acquires a capital. The capture of Jerusalem and its appointment as capital could be regarded as an astute move by David and his henchmen. Jerusalem was near enough to the border between the Southern tribes and those of the North and could, therefore, function as a unifying factor for all twelve tribes. It was viewed as such by the Chronicler. For him it was the heart centre of the people; the place where the Temple was to be; the place, above all, of the presence of God in the midst of his people. We in the Western world have lost that sense of the sacredness of place which Judaism and Islam still have. We find it difficult to appreciate the emotion of the Jew murmuring at the Passover ceremony down through the ages: "Next year in Jerusalem," though he knows he may never set eyes on the city.

The Chronicler's account of how it all began is almost laconic in its matter of factness. The extent of the city which David built on the site of the Jebusite stronghold was very small in comparison with what it later was to become. The chart opposite will show the size of the city at various stages of its development.

The city of David was on the site of the old Jebusite stronghold on the south eastern corner of the present Old City but outside the walls. The "Millo" mentioned in the text has always puzzled historians but recent archeological investigation in the area would seem to imply that it was a filling done to enlarge the saddle of land to the north. This would pave the way for the further expansion northward in

---

The shaded area on each map represents the inhabited section of Jerusalem at each historical age. 1. Large enclosed area indicates the walled city today with the Temple courtyard in the lower right. The wall was built by Suleiman in 1539-42; the shaded area points out the city in the time of David. 2. Age of Solomon and the construction of the Temple. 3. Age of Josiah. 4. Age of Nehemiah, up to the conquest of Alexander the Great. 5. Age of Alexander Janneus 103-76 B.C. 6a. Age of Herod the Great. 6b. A little before the destruction of the Temple in 70 A.D. 7. Age of Justinian.

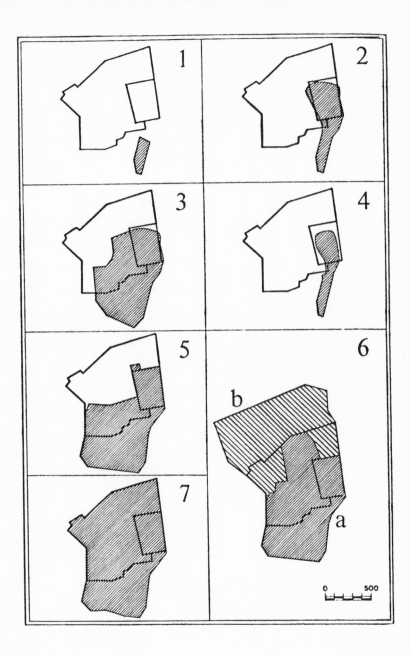

Solomon's time. The population during David's reign was only about 2,000. This had risen to over 5,000 by Solomon's time and to 70,000 before the Exile, but it probably had fallen again to less than 5,000 in the Chronicler's own day. Before the destruction of the Second Temple in A.D. 67 it was over 80,000. Through all the fluctuations of history, the city which David made his own remained at the heart of Judaism. (Cf. *Old Testament Message* 6 for a fuller account of the place of Jerusalem in Israel's history).

David's Warriors
11:10-47

[10]Now these are the chiefs of David's mighty men, who gave him strong support in his kingdom, together with all Israel, to make him king, according to the word of the Lord concerning Israel. [11]This is an account of David's mighty men; Jashobeam, a Hachmonite, was chief of the three; he wielded his spear against three hundred whom he slew at one time.

[12]And next to him among the three mighty men was Eleazar the son of Dodo, the Ahohite. [13]He was with David at Pasdammim when the Philistines were gathered there for battle. There was a plot of ground full of barley, and the men fled from the Philistines. [14]But he took his stand in the midst of the plot, and defended it, and slew the Philistines; and the Lord saved them by a great victory.

[15]Three of the thirty chief men went down to the rock to David at the cave of Adullam, when the army of Philistines was encamped in the valley of Rephaim. [16]David was then in the stronghold; and the garrison of the Philistines was then at Bethlehem. [17]And David said longingly, "O that some one would give me water to drink from the well of Bethlehem which is by the gate!" [18]Then the three mighty men broke through the camp of the Philistines, and drew water out of the well of Bethlehem which was by the gate, and took and brought it to David. But David would not drink of it; he poured it out to the Lord, [19]and

said, "Far be it from me before my God that I should do this. Shall I drink the lifeblood of these men? For at the risk of their lives they brought it." Therefore he would not drink it. These things did the three mighty men.

Joab had been mentioned in the previous section as the chief of David's fighting men. It is obvious that David was the kind of leader who drew brave men to him and the remainder of chapter eleven gives lists of these men in true Chronicler fashion. First mentioned are a group called the "three" who seemed to have had a position apart but only two of them and their exploits are actually outlined. Next comes the "thirty" who were probably the most noteworthy of David's warriors in his early days. The make-up of the thirty is largely the same as that in 2 Samuel (23:24-39) and the names are chiefly from David's home territory in Judah with a sprinkling from the other tribes. The Chronicler adds a further sixteen men to the list of the thirty, probably to emphasize David's rising popularity.

An episode in which some of the thirty tried to satisfy a whim of David's is told in some detail (11:15-19). This is one of the few stories from David's earlier life which the Chronicler has preserved. He did so possibly because of the favourable light it sheds on David's attitude to God and to the lives of his followers.

The Tribes Rally to David
12:1-22

12 Now these are the men who came to David at Ziklag, while he could not move about freely because of Saul the son of Kish; and they were among the mighty men who helped him in war. ²They were bowmen, and could shoot arrows and sling stones with either the right or the left hand; they were Benjaminites, Saul's kinsmen....

¹⁶And some of the men of Benjamin and Judah came to the stronghold to David. ¹⁷David went out to meet them and said to them, "If you have come to me in friendship to help me, my heart will be knit to you; but if to betray me

to my adversaries, although there is no wrong in my hands, then may the God of our fathers see and rebuke you." [18]Then the Spirit came upon Amasai, chief of the thirty, and he said,

> "We are yours, O David;
>   and with you, O son of Jesse!
> Peace, peace to you,
>   and peace to your helpers!
> For your God helps you."

Then David received them, and made them officers of his troops.

David's sojorn in Ziglag (12:1, 20; cf. 4:30) belonged to the period of his life when, to escape Saul, he went over to the Philistines, one of whose kings gave him Ziglag as his own possession (cf. 1 Sam 27:1-7). Historically it was the lowest point of David's career but the Chronicler's portrayal of the period presents David's star so clearly in ascendant that members of Saul's tribe, the Benjaminites, cross over to him.

David had plenty of reason to be suspicious of newcomers since he had been previously betrayed (cf. 1 Sam 21). The commitment of his cause to God here puts into words what had been apparent in many of the actions of his rise to power (e.g. 1 Sam 24:11-15). Amasai's inspired reply gives him assurance. The prosaic translation: "Then the spirit of the Lord came upon Amasai," does not do justice to the underlying text where what is said literally is that the spirit "put on", "clothed himself in" Amasai, much in the way one puts on a coat. This idea of inspiration is to be found elsewhere in the Bible (cf. Judg 6:34; 2 Chron 24:20). The beautiful snatch of Hebrew poetry which follows wishes David the best of all possible gifts: *Shalom*. Again the Hebrew word has much richer connotations than the English word, *peace*. It is not just the absence of war but the fullness of well-being and of plenty. David would have this because God was on his side.

Coronation Feast at Hebron
12:23-40

23These are the numbers of the divisions of the armed troops, who came to David in Hebron, to turn the kingdom of Saul over to him, according to the word of the Lord. 24The men of Judah bearing shield and spear were six thousand eight hundred armed troops. 25Of the Simeonites, mighty men of valor for war, seven thousand one hundred. 26Of the Levites four thousand six hundred....

38All these, men of war, arrayed in battle order, came to Hebron with full intent to make David king over all Israel; likewise all the rest of Israel were of a single mind to make David king. 39And they were there with David for three days, eating and drinking, for their brethren had made preparation for them. 40And also their neighbors, from as far as Issachar and Zebulun and Naphtali, came bringing food on asses and on camels and on mules and on oxen, abundant provisions of meal, cakes of figs, clusters of raisins, and wine and oil, oxen and sheep, for there was joy in Israel.

This section is the sequel to 11:1-3 and completes the account of the kingship of David at Hebron. All the tribes are represented at the installation of David as king by the presence of their mighty warriors. The whole scene is more idealistic than real and the unrealistic numbers have to be seen in this light. The point is again being made that "all Israel" must be present at the coronation feast of David since he was the one, par excellence, who gathered the people together as a whole (see Intro. p. 7).

The "joy in Israel" as the coronation took place is not the ordinary joy of celebration. Elsewhere in Chronicles it has religious connotations (cf. 1 Chron 29:20-22; 2 Chron 7:8-10; 30:23). It is the same joy which even to this day is present in the celebration of the Jewish New Year when the orthodox Jew dances with the joy of the Torah. It is said that even in the concentration camps in the Second World

War, Jews poignantly fulfilled the rites of this joyful festival in their devotion to their Law, the Torah.

The Removal of the Ark
13:1-14

13 David consulted with the commanders of thousands and of hundreds, with every leader. [2]And David said to all the assembly of Israel, "If it seems good to you, and if it is the will of the Lord our God, let us send abroad to our brethren who remain in all the land of Israel, and with them to the priests and Levites in the cities that have pasture lands, that they may come together to us. [3]Then let us bring again the ark of our God to us; for we neglected it in the days of Saul." [4]All the assembly agreed to do so, for the thing was right in the eyes of all the people. . . .

[9]And when they came to the threshing floor of Chidon, Uzzah put out his hand to hold the ark, for the oxen stumbled. [10]And the anger of the Lord was kindled against Uzzah; and he smote him because he put forth his hand to the ark; and he died there before God. [11]And David was angry because the Lord had broken forth upon Uzzah; and that place is called Perezuzza to this day. [12]And David was afraid of God that day; and he said, "How can I bring the ark of God home to me?" [13]So David did not take the ark home into the city of David, but took it aside to the house of Obededom the Gittite. [14]And the ark of God remained with the household of Obededom in his house three months; and the Lord blessed the household of Obededom and all that he had.

This chapter provides an example of the rearrangement of material by the Chronicler to suit his own preoccupations. In 2 Samuel the removal of the Ark follows on details concerning David's setting up house in Jerusalem and his military activities against the Philistines (cf. 1 Chron 14:3-17). For the Chronicler the most important, and therefore the first, action of his early career in Jerusalem was the care of the Ark of the Covenant which had been neglected by Saul. In such an important endeavour, "all Israel" must again be present (vv. 2, 5, 6; see intro. p. 7).

The Ark was a chest made of precious wood, often considered a throne for God or regarded as his footstool. According to tradition, it contained the tablets of the Law given to Moses on Mount Sinai. The reason for this belief stems from the Near Eastern practice, verified by archeological finds, of burying covenants or other documents under the images of the gods. The Ark was a symbol of God's presence with his people and of his concern for them.

First associated with the period of wandering in the desert (cf. Ex 25:10-22; Deut 10:1-5), it had a chequered career during the period of conquest and consolidation (cf. Josh 3-4; 1 Sam 3-5). By mentioning Saul's neglect of the Ark, the Chronicler may be hinting at the underlying reason for his failure. David's concern is accordingly highlighted. The first attempt at bringing the Ark to Jerusalem failed because someone other than the Levites had the intention of touching the Ark. In the Samuel account, Uzziah actually holds the Ark; it is not clear that he did so in Chronicles but even the intention was enough. It is difficult for us to appreciate such stern judgment but it comes from a period when devotion to rubrics was part of a survival mentality.

David Settles Down in Jerusalem; His Victories
14:1-17

14 And Hiram king of Tyre sent messengers to David, and cedar trees, also masons and carpenters to build a house for him. ²And David perceived that the Lord had established him king over Israel, and that his kingdom was highly exalted for the sake of his people Israel.

³And David took more wives in Jerusalem, and David begot more sons and daughters. ⁴These are the names of the children whom he had in Jerusalem: Shammua, Shobab, Nathan, Solomon, ⁵Ibhar, Elishua, Elpelet, ⁶Nogah, Nepheg, Japhia, ⁷Elishama, Beeliada, and

Eliphelet.

⁸When the Philistines heard that David had been anointed king over all Israel, all the Philistines went up in search of David; and David heard of it and went out against them. ⁹Now the Philistines had come and made a raid in the valley of Rephaim. ¹⁰And David inquired of God, "Shall I go up against the Philistines? Wilt thou give them into my hand?" And the Lord said to him, "Go up, and I will give them into your hand." ¹¹And he went up to Baalperazim, and David defeated them there....

¹⁶And David did as God commanded him, and they smote the Philistine army from Gibeon to Gezer. ¹⁷And the fame of David went out into all lands, and the Lord brought the fear of him upon all nations.

David becomes firmly established in Jerusalem. His prosperity is shown by the gifts of materials for palace building from a foreign king and by the increase in his family. Solomon's name is included in the list of sons born to David in Jerusalem without any mention of his mother, Bathsheba, or of how David came to marry her. The story of David's adultery and the murder of Uriah, Bathsheba's husband, would have sullied the character sketch which the Chronicler supplied of his hero (see p. 28).

David in Hebron had not proved a threat to the Philistines but David as king of "all Israel", firmly entrenched in Jerusalem was a very different matter. The remainder of the chapter recounts their unsuccessful attempts to bring him down. Unsuccessful, for the Chronicler, because David was careful to consult God before going into battle. David's prosperity was not due to any efforts of his own but rather to the actions of God on his behalf. David himself is portrayed as being aware of this and aware also that it is not for his own sake that he is given the kingship but "for the sake of his people Israel" (cf. v.2). As a result of his victories over the Philistines David becomes a force to be reckoned with in the power politics of his time.

THE ARK COMES TO JERUSALEM
15—17.

15 David built houses for himself in the city of David; and he prepared a place for the ark of God, and pitched a tent for it. ²Then David said, "No one but the Levites may carry the ark of God, for the Lord chose them to carry the ark of the Lord and to minister to him for ever." ³And David assembled all Israel at Jerusalem, to bring up the ark of the Lord to its place, which he had prepared for it. ⁴And David gathered together the sons of Aaron and the Levites. . . .

¹⁴So the priests and the Levites sanctified themselves to bring up the ark of the Lord, the God of Israel. ¹⁵And the Levites carried the ark of God upon their shoulders with the poles, as Moses had commanded according to the word of the Lord.

The central concern of the Chronicler is the organisation of David's kingdom both in civil administration and in religious matters. Now that the former has rather summarily been dealt with, he turns his mind resolutely to what for him is far more important. In this central section of First Chronicles the Ark, the religious symbol par excellence of the people, finally reaches Jerusalem. The Chronicler would have us realise that when the proper cultic personnel (the Levites; see Intro. p.5) handle the Ark and when they do so in the proper way (on poles as prescribed and not unceremoniously on a cart), then no harm comes to anyone. Speaking to the Levites the Chronicler has David say: "Because you did not carry it the first time, the Lord our God broke forth upon us, because we did not care for it in the way that is ordained" (1 Chron 15:13).

We may consider such preoccupation legalistic, or even fatalistic, but for a people afraid of losing its identity, as the post-exilic community was, obedience to ritual and due order was an important virtue to cultivate as a necessary pre-requisite for survival.

The Chronicler's account of the translation of the Ark is, therefore, liturgical in character whereas the underlying account in 2 Samuel (cf. 2 Sam 6:12-20) is much more political. It was an astute political move on David's part to have the religious symbol of the people firmly anchored in the new capital city. This would ensure the unity of religion and politics. The unifying character of the event is also stressed by again mentioning the presence of "all Israel" in Jerusalem for the occasion.

Bringing the Ark Up with Rejoicing
15:16—16:3

> [16]David also commanded the chiefs of the Levites to appoint their brethren as the singers who should play loudly on musical instruments, on harps and lyres and cymbals, to raise sounds of joy. . . .
> [23]Berechiah and Elkanah were to be gatekeepers for the ark. [24]Shebaniah, Joshaphat, Nethanel, Amasai, Zechariah, Benaiah, and Eliezer, the priests, should blow the trumpets before the ark of God. Obededom and Jehiah also were to be gatekeepers for the ark.
> [25]So David and the elders of Israel, and the commanders of thousands, went to bring up the ark of the covenant of the Lord from the house of Obededom with rejoicing. [26]And because God helped the Levites who were carrying the ark of the covenant of the Lord, they sacrificed seven bulls and seven rams. [27]David was clothed with a robe of fine linen, as also were all the Levites who were carrying the ark, and the singers, and Chenaniah the leader of the music of the singers; and David wore a linen ephod. [28]So all Israel brought up the ark of the covenant of the Lord with shouting, to the sound of the horn, trumpets, and cymbals, and made loud music on harps and lyres.
> [29]And as the ark of the covenant of the Lord came to the city of David, Michal the daughter of Saul looked out the window, and saw King David dancing and making merry; and she despised him in her heart.

When they were finished carrying the Ark, the Levites were to function before it as singers and gatekeepers. Such functions, of course, belonged to the time of the Second Temple rather than to that of David (see Intro. pp. 5, 6). The use of singing and dancing in the bringing up of the Ark at the time of David was probably similar to that practised on more ordinary occasions such as can still be seen today in Arab villages in Palestine, for example on the occasion of the completion of a new house. David's emotional display is toned down somewhat in comparison with the 2 Samuel account (cf. 2 Sam 6:12-23). Likewise the reaction of his wife, Michal, is not so much because she is disgusted at David making an exhibition of himself as in 2 Samuel but because, being a daughter of Saul, she has a wrong attitude to the Ark (see p. 37).

The tradition that David was interested in music is very strong at every level of the Bible and the setting up of musical guilds may indeed go back to his time. The elaborate use of music in Israelite liturgy, however, is only evident from the time of the Second Temple. The instruments mentioned here, the *nevel*, the *kinnor* and the *meziltayim*, appear elsewhere in Chronicles as instruments of the cult (e.g. 1 Chron 25:1); according to later Jewish sources, they formed part of the Temple orchestra in post-exilic times.

The *nevel* was a type of lyre corresponding somewhat to our harp. According to Josephus, the Jewish historian of Roman times, it had twelve strings and was played by plucking with the fingers. The *kinnor*, the lyre, was the most important instrument of Semitic peoples and was said to have been the instrument of David. According to Josephus, it had ten strings and was sounded with a plectrum. The *meziltayim* were cymbals, probably made of bronze in the form of plates with a central hollow boss. Also mentioned are the *shofar* and the *hazozerah*. The former was a ram's horn and was used as a signal especially in time of war; the latter was a trumpet and was a Temple instrument blown only by the priests. The *shofar* is the only instrument to have survived in Jewish religious usage. It is still used today in synagogue services especially on *Rosh ha-Shanah*, the feast of the Jewish New Year.

Thanksgiving for the Ark's Presence in Jerusalem
16:4-36

⁷Then on that day David first appointed that thanksgiving be sung to the Lord by Asaph and his brethren.

⁸O give thanks to the Lord, call on his name,
   make known his deeds among the peoples!
⁹Sing to him, sing praises to him,
   tell of all his wonderful works!
¹⁰Glory in his holy name;
   let the hearts of those who seek the Lord rejoice!
¹¹Seek the Lord and his strength,
   seek his presence continually!
¹²Remember the wonderful works that he has done,
   the wonders he wrought, the judgments he uttered,
¹³O offspring of Abraham his servant,
   sons of Jacob, his chosen ones!
¹⁴He is the Lord our God;
   his judgments are in all the earth.
¹⁵He is mindful of his covenant for ever,
   of the word that he commanded, for a thousand
   generations,
¹⁶the covenant which he made with Abraham,
   his sworn promise to Isaac,
¹⁷which he confirmed as a statute to Jacob,
   as an everlasting covenant to Israel,
¹⁸saying, "To you I will give the land of Canaan,
   as your portion for an inheritance.". . .
³⁴O give thanks to the Lord, for he is good;
   for his steadfast love endures for ever!
³⁵Say also:
   "Deliver us, O God of our salvation,
      and gather and save us from among the nations,
   that we may give thanks to thy holy name,
      and glory in thy praise.

³⁶Blessed be the Lord, the God of Israel,
    from everlasting to everlasting!"
Then all the people said "Amen!" and praised the Lord.

The coming of the Ark to Jerusalem initiated a new era in the life of the people. This is emphasized by speaking of the Ark as the "Ark of the covenant of the Lord" (16:6, 37). What God had promised in the great covenants of the past, to Abraham, Isaac, Jacob and Moses, was not fulfilled in David's bringing of the Ark to Jerusalem. The natural reaction of the Chronicler is a great hymn of thanksgiving and praise to God for his goodness.

To convey his sense of praise and thanksgiving, the Chronicler uses passages from three psalms which are known to us from the Psalter: Pss 105[104]: 1-15; 96[95]: 1-13; 106 [105]:1, 47, 48. These are psalms which speak of the wonders of God's action in the past by his deliverance of his people. The Chronicler does not go into detail about these past actions, omitting such of Pss 105 and 106 where they are outlined, but significantly keeping mention of the covenant from Ps 105, a covenant possessed by a people "few in number" and "wandering from nation to nation." (cf. 2 Chron 6:14; 15:12, Ezra 10:3; Neh 1:5).

Thanksgiving for the bringing up of the ark is not the only, nor even the primary purpose of the Chronicler in combining these three psalms (see Intro. p. 3). His main preoccupation, as always, is to give hope to the people of his own time. There is much in these verses which speaks of deliverance and so the Chronicler wishes to reassure the post-exilic community, a people "few in number", lost among the world powers of the time. God is still with them, the same God who rescued his people from of old and who made covenant with them in the past and again with David. He is the God who will judge the earth and vindicate his chosen messengers.

The great liturgical shout, "Amen" is included at the end of the prayer. The "Amen" was a symbol of the people's assent to what had been recited in the liturgy and was accompanied by the banging of cymbals and other instruments. It was a much more dramatic affair, therefore, than the sober "Amen" in present liturgical usage.

Worship at Gibeon
16:37-43

[37]So David left Asaph and his brethren there before the ark of the covenant of the Lord to minister continually before the ark as each day required, [38]and also Obededom and his sixty-eight brethren; while Obededom, the son of Jeduthun, and Hosah were to be gatekeepers. [39]And he left Zadok the priest and his brethren the priests before the tabernacle of the Lord in the high place that was at Gibeon, [40]to offer burnt offerings to the Lord upon the altar of burnt offering continually morning and evening, according to all that is written in the law of the Lord which he commanded Israel.

The end of chapter sixteen makes provision for the continual ministry before the Ark but also adds the interesting observation that sacrifices were still being offered before the "tabernacle of the Lord" in the high place at Gibeon. The 2 Samuel source (cf. 2 Sam 6) makes no mention of the tabernacle at Gibeon but the Chronicler is firm in his witness to two great centres of religion at this stage of Israel's history and elsewhere in the Samuel-Kings complex, Gibeon is seen as a great "high place" (cf. 1 Kings 3:4).

The tabernacle goes back to the idea of the Tent of Meeting in the desert where God was said to speak to Moses "face to face" (Ex 33:11); it stood for the presence of God in giving direction to his people. The actual tent could embody the idea of a portable sanctuary, of the kind which Bedouin in the desert carry with them to this day. The accounts of the relationship between Ark and tabernacle vary in different parts of the Bible. The text here in Chronicles presumes a tradition in which they were separate.

Nathan's Prophecy to David and David's Prayer
17:1-27

17 Now when David dwelt in his house, David said to Nathan the prophet, "Behold, I dwell in a house of cedar, but the ark of the covenant of the Lord is under a tent." ²And Nathan said to David, "Do all that is in your heart, for God is with you."

³But that same night the word of the Lord came to Nathan, ⁴"Go and tell my servant David, 'Thus says the Lord: You shall not build me a house to dwell in. ⁵For I have not dwelt in a house since the day I led up Israel to this day, but I have gone from tent to tent and from dwelling to dwelling. ⁶In all places where I have moved with all Israel, did I speak a word with any of the judges of Israel, whom I commanded to shepherd my people, saying, "Why have you not built me a house of cedar?" ' ⁷Now therefore thus shall you say to my servant David, 'Thus says the Lord of hosts, I took you from the pasture, from following the sheep, that you should be prince over my people Israel; ⁸and I have been with you wherever you went, and have cut off all your enemies from before you; and I will make for you a name, like the name of the great ones of the earth. ⁹And I will appoint a place for my people Israel, and will plant them, that they may dwell in their own place, and be disturbed no more; and violent men shall waste them no more, as formerly, ¹⁰from the time that I appointed judges over my people Israel; and I will subdue all your enemies. Moreover I declare to you that the Lord will build you a house. ¹¹When your days are fulfilled to go to be with your fathers, I will raise up your offspring after you, one of your own sons, and I will establish his kingdom. ¹²He shall build a house for me, and I will establish his throne for ever. ¹³I will be his father, and he shall be my son; I will not take my steadfast love from him, as I took it from him who was before you, ¹⁴but I will confirm him in my house and in my kingdom for ever and his throne shall be established for ever.' " ¹⁵In accordance with all these words, and in accordance with

all this vision, Nathan spoke to David.

¹⁶Then King David went in and sat before the Lord, and said, "Who am I, O Lord God, and what is my house, that thou hast brought me thus far? ¹⁷And this was a small thing in thy eyes, O God; thou hast also spoken of thy servant's house for a great while to come, and hast shown me future generations, O Lord God! ¹⁸And what more can David say to thee for honoring thy servant? For thou knowest thy servant. ¹⁹For thy servant's sake, O Lord, and according to thy own heart, thou hast wrought all this greatness, in making known all these great things. ²⁰There is none like thee, O Lord, and there is no God besides thee, according to all that we have heard with our ears. ²¹What other nation on earth is like thy people Israel, whom God went to redeem to be his people, making for thyself a name for great and terrible things, in driving out nations before thy people whom thou didst redeem from Egypt? ²²And thou didst make thy people Israel to be thy people for ever; and thou, O Lord, didst become their God. ²³And now, O Lord, let the word which thou hast spoken concerning thy servant and concerning his house be established for ever, and do as thou hast spoken; ²⁴and thy name will be established and magnified for ever, saying, 'The Lord of hosts, the God of Israel, is Israel's God,' and the house of thy servant David will be established before thee. ²⁵For thou, my God, hast revealed to thy servant that thou wilt build a house for him; therefore thy servant has found courage to pray before thee. ²⁶And now, O Lord, thou art God, and thou hast promised this good thing to thy servant; ²⁷now therefore may it please thee to bless the house of thy servant, that it may continue for ever before thee; for what thou, O Lord, hast blessed is blessed for ever."

David's desire to build a more permanent home for the Ark is the background to this chapter. For once, the source in 2 Samuel is followed very closely though there are some characteristic changes. For example, 2 Sam 7:11-16 reads:

"Moreover the Lord declares to you that the Lord will make you a house. When your days are fulfilled and you lie down with your fathers, I will raise up your offspring after you, who shall come forth from your body and I will establish his kingdom...And *your* house and *your* kingdom shall be made sure forever before me; your throne shall be established forever." If this is compared with 1 Chron 17:10-14 above, it will be seen that the first part corresponds very well with the mention of God building a dynasty for David. It is clear, then, that the messianic character of the text in Chronicles comes from the source (see Intro. p. 4).

At the end of the passage, however, the emphasis changes since the Chronicler has: "I will confirm him in *my* house and in *my* kingdom forever." The change of pronoun emphasises that, for the Chronicler, David's and Solomon's rule was merely a participation in kingship; the real king of Israel was God himself (cf. 2 Chron 9:8). Likewise the "my house" in Chronicles refers to the Temple in the building of which David and Solomon would be instrumental. The preoccupation of the Chronicler with the Temple is evident, therefore, even in his handling of so royal a passage as the oracle of Nathan.

The prayer of David bears witness to the realisation of each successive age that David was a man who, for all his faults, always showed trust and dependence on God. It again underlines the fact that the king in Israel must never rule from his own power but only from that of God. His task was to rule a covenanted people who had known the power of their God in the past. That power was manifested anew by the choice of David as king and by the establishment of his kingdom.

THE EXPANSION AND ADMINISTRATION OF DAVID'S KINGDOM
18:1—21:30

18 After this David defeated the Philistines and

subdued them, and he took Gath and its villages out of the hand of the Philistines.

²And he defeated Moab, and the Moabites became servants to David and brought tribute.

³David also defeated Hadadezer king of Zobah, toward Hamath, as he went to set up his monument at the river Euphrates. ⁴And David took from him a thousand chariots, seven thousand horsemen, and twenty thousand foot soldiers; and David hamstrung all the chariot horses, but left enough for a hundred chariots. ⁵And when the Syrians of Damascus came to help Hadadezer king of Zobah, David slew twenty-two thousand men of the Syrians. ⁶Then David put garrisons in Syria of Damascus; and the Syrians became servants to David, and brought tribute. And the Lord gave victory to David wherever he went. ⁷And David took the shields of gold which were carried by the servants of Hadadezer, and brought them to Jerusalem. ⁸And from Tibhath and from Cun, cities of Hadadezer, David took very much bronze; with it Solomon made the bronze sea and the pillars and the vessels of bronze. . . .

¹⁴So David reigned over all Israel; and he administered justice and equity to all his people. ¹⁵And Joab the son of Zeruiah was over the army; and Jehoshaphat the son of Ahilud was recorder; ¹⁶and Zadok the son of Ahitub and Ahimelech the son of Abiathar were priests; and Shavsha was secretary; ¹⁷and Benaiah the son of Jehoiada was over the Cherethites and the Pelethites; and David's sons were the chief officials in the service of the king.

A summary of the foreign wars in which David was engaged now follows. These have been collected from scattered sections of 2 Samuel, giving the impression of an expansionist policy at the expense of neighbouring kingdoms. The Philistines are brought into line to the west (18:1; 20:4-8; cf. 14:8-17) though not wholly conquered. Israel's traditional enemies to the East Edom, Moab and Ammon, fall foul of David (18:2, 12-13; 19:1-20:3) while, to the

North, the Aramean states are either subdued or treat David with a wholesome respect (18:3-11; 19:10-19). The map on the following page gives an indication of the extent of David's expansion.

In 2 Samuel these accounts of foreign wars are interspersed with the increasing failure of David in domestic battles: the affair with Bathsheba (2 Sam 11, 12), the incest and subsequent murder of his son, Amnon (2 Sam 13), and the revolt of his favourite son, Absalom (2 Sam 15-19). David is idealised in Chronicles, and the Chronicler is not concerned with his private life; only his public actions merit attention in his eyes. Even such acts as his kindness to Saul's family is omitted as were previous relations between Saul and David.

The picture of David which emerges from these chapters is that of a great conqueror. He accepts victories as coming from the hand of God, however, and not merely as the result of his own prowess. The wealth acquired in conquest is to be wholly dedicated to God, much in the way of the dedication of booty in the holy war concept of earlier historical writing; with this difference, however, that the booty is not now destroyed but given over for the building of the Temple. Even in recounting events of war, then, the Chronicler's preoccupation with the Temple is easily apparent.

David needed to update the old tribal system of administration to cater for such a vastly expanded territory. A short list of the most important posts in the new administration is given in the passage. The king himself was chief justice. In the East, at least in theory, the administration of justice was always a jealously preserved prerogative of rulership. The ideal king in Israel should be seen to administer justice (cf. 1 Kings 3:16-28; Is 11:4; Ps 72[71]). To this day, every subject has the right of approach to his leader, be he desert sheik, crowned head or eastern rite bishop, in order to obtain justice.

Next to the king was the army commander, Joab, who indeed, as can be seen from the accounts of the wars detailed in these chapters, was largely responsible for the expansion

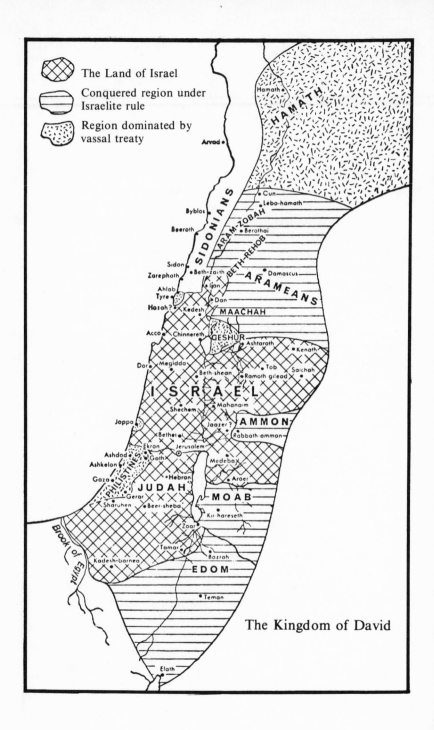

The Land of Israel

Conquered region under Israelite rule

Region dominated by vassal treaty

HAMATH

Hamath

Arvad

Cun

Byblos

Lebo-hamath

ARAM-ZOBAH

Beeroth

Berothai

BETH-REHOB

Sidon

Beth-zaith

Damascus

Zarephath

Ijon

ARAMEANS

Ahlab

Dan

Tyre

Hosah?

Kedesh

MAACHAH

Acco

Chinnereth

GESHUR

Ashtaroth

Kenath

Dor

Megiddo

Tob

Saichah

Beth-shean

Ramoth gilead

ISRAEL

Shechem

Mahanaim

Joppa

Jaazer?

AMMON

Bethel

Rabbath-amman

Ekron

Jerusalem

Ashdod

Gath

Medeba

Ashkelon

Aroer

Gaza

Hebron

JUDAH

MOAB

Gerar

Sharuhen

Beer-sheba

Kir-hareseth

Zoar

Tamar

Bozrah

Kadesh-barnea

EDOM

Brook of Egypt

Teman

Elath

SIDONIANS

PHILISTINES

The Kingdom of David

of the kingdom. Also mentioned in connection with the army is the chief of the king's personal bodyguard, the need for security being the price of fame even at that early date in history. The office of *recorder* has caused much speculation among scholars. It is quite likely that David modelled his administration on that of Egypt; this official would probably correspond to the royal herald mentioned in many Egyptian records. A title such as "Chief of Protocol" would probably be the modern equivalent. Shavsha (18:16) was royal secretary, being the king's private secretary as well as fulfilling the duties of Secretary of State. Responsible for all correspondence and for Temple collections (cf. 2 Kings 12:10-11) he played an important part in public affairs.

Also mentioned in the list of administrators are the priests, Zadok and Ahimelech, showing how close religious functions were to the political. Indeed in 2 Samuel the notice of administrative personnel ends with the mention of David's sons as priests (2 Sam 8:18). The Chronicler, of course, could not tolerate this, since by his time all priests had to be Levites, so he changed the text to read: "and David's sons were the chief officials in the service of the king."

The Taking of the Census
21:1—22:1

21   Satan stood up against Israel, and incited David to number Israel. [2]So David said to Joab and the commanders of the army, "Go, number Israel, from Beersheba to Dan, and bring me a report, that I may know their number." [3]But Joab said, "May the Lord add to his people a hundred times as many as they are! Are they not, my lord the king, all of them my lord's servants? Why then should my lord require this? Why should he bring guilt upon Israel?" [4]But the king's word prevailed against Joab. So Joab departed and went throughout all Israel, and came back to Jerusalem. . . .

⁷But God was displeased with this thing, and he smote Israel. ⁸And David said to God, "I have sinned greatly in that I have done this thing. But now, I pray thee, take away the iniquity of thy servant; for I have done very foolishly.". . .

¹⁴So the Lord sent a pestilence upon Israel; and there fell seventy thousand men of Israel. ¹⁵And God sent the angel to Jerusalem to destroy it; but when he was about to destroy it, the Lord saw, and he repented of the evil; and he said to the destroying angel, "It is enough; now stay your hand." And the angel of the Lord was standing by the threshing floor of Ornan the Jebusite. ¹⁶And David lifted his eyes and saw the angel of the Lord standing between earth and heaven, and in his hand a drawn sword stretched out over Jerusalem. Then David and the elders, clothed in sackcloth, fell upon their faces. ¹⁷And David said to God, "Was it not I who gave command to number the people? It is I who have sinned and done very wickedly. But these sheep, what have they done? Let thy hand, I pray thee, O Lord my God, be against me and against my father's house; but let not the plague be upon thy people."

¹⁸Then the angel of the Lord commanded Gad to say to David that David should go up and rear an altar to the Lord on the threshing floor of Ornan the Jebusite. ¹⁹So David went up at Gad's word, which he had spoken in the name of the Lord. ²⁰Now Ornan was threshing wheat; he turned and saw the angel, and his four sons who were with him hid themselves. ²¹As David came to Ornan, Ornan looked and saw David and went forth from the threshing floor, and did obeisance to David with his face to the ground. ²²And David said to Ornan, "Give me the site of the threshing floor that I may build on it an altar to the Lord—give it to me at its full price—that the plague may be averted from the people." ²³Then Ornan said to David, "Take it; and let my lord the king do what seems good to him; see, I give the oxen for burnt offerings, and the threshing sledges for the wood, and the wheat for a

cereal offering. I give it all." [24]But King David said to Ornan, "No, but I will buy it for the full price; I will not take for the Lord what is yours, nor offer burnt offerings which cost me nothing." [25]So David paid Ornan six hundred shekels of gold by weight for the site.[26]And David built there an altar to the Lord and presented burnt offerings and peace offerings, and called upon the Lord, and he answered him with fire from heaven upon the altar of burnt offering. [27]Then the Lord commanded the angel; and he put his sword back into its sheath.

[28]At that time, when David saw that the Lord had answered him at the threshing floor of Ornan the Jebusite, he made his sacrifices there. . . .

22 [1]Then David said, "Here shall be the house of the Lord God and here the altar of burnt offering for Israel."

Up to this point, the Chronicler avoided recounting any of the earlier stories which portrayed David as a sinner but, at last, he is forced into doing so because the story of David's taking of a census of the people provides the backdrop for the acquiring of the land on which the Temple was to be built. It is interesting, though, that when he does have to speak of David as sinning it is a sin of mistrust that he records. For him this is what is involved in the taking of a census. The Satan at the beginning of the story stands in the line of the devil's advocate type of figure to be seen in Job 1, 2 and Zech 3:1. His function is basically to test David: will he trust wholly in God or will he, like other kings, put his trust in military power and so find out by a census on what strength he can rely?

David fails the test but this is not the end for the Chronicler because, by his repentance, he is forgiven (see Intro. p. 8) and the event is turned into a blessing since it involves the purchase of the site on which the Temple was to be built. In the bargaining for the site between David and the Jebusite there are many parallels with the story of Abraham. The Chronicler is deliberately equating the Temple site with the first bit of land owned by the ancestors of Israel, therefore he tells the story in terms of Abraham's bargaining for land in Genesis 23. The text is also linked with Genesis 22 which is the story of the sacrifice of Isaac. The mountain on which Isaac was sacrificed was a mountain of Moriah and the Chronicler will call the Temple site, *Mount Moriah* in 2 Chron 3:1. The most likely meaning of Moriah is "the Lord will see" (cf. Gen 22:14 — Jerusalem Bible translation) and in 1 Chron 21:15, the text says that "the Lord saw." This is a very good example of the midrashic tendencies of the Chronicler (see Intro. p. 3) where earlier texts of the Bible are interpreted to explain later ones and to bring out their significance for the writer's own time. It is interesting to note also that the Chronicler is going back behind the Exodus to show David as fulfilling in an unique way the promises made to the Patriarchs (see p. 15).

PREPARATION FOR TEMPLE CONSTRUCTION
22:2—29:30

²David commanded to gather together the aliens who were in the land of Israel, and he set stonecutters to prepare dressed stones for building the house of God. ³David also provided great stores of iron for nails for the doors of the gates and for clamps, as well as bronze in quantities beyond weighing, ⁴and cedar timbers without number; for the Sidonians and Tyrians brought great quantities of cedar to David. ⁵For David said, "Solomon my son is young and inexperienced, and the house that is to be built for the Lord must be exceedingly magnificent, of fame and glory throughout all lands; I will therefore make preparation for it." So David provided materials in great quantity before his death.

⁶Then he called for Solomon his son, and charged him to build a house for the Lord, the God of Israel. ⁷David said to Solomon, "My son, I had it in my heart to build a house to the name of the Lord my God. ⁸But the word of the Lord came to me, saying, 'You have shed much blood

and have waged great wars; you shall not build a house to my name, because you have shed so much blood before me upon the earth. [9]Behold, a son shall be born to you; he shall be a man of peace. I will give him peace from all his enemies round about; for his name shall be Solomon, and I will give peace and quiet to Israel in his days. [10]He shall build a house for my name. He shall be my son, and I will be his father, and I will establish his royal throne in Israel for ever.' [11]Now, my son, the Lord be with you, so that you may succeed in building the house of the Lord your God, as he has spoken concerning you. [12]Only, may the Lord grant you discretion and understanding, that when he gives you charge over Israel you may keep the law of the Lord your God. [13]Then you will prosper if you are careful to observe the statutes and the ordinances which the Lord commanded Moses for Israel. Be strong, and of good courage. Fear not; be not dismayed. . . .

Arise and be doing! The Lord be with you!"

[17]David also commanded all the leaders of Israel to help Solomon his son, saying, [18]"Is not the Lord your God with you? And has he not given you peace on every side? For he has delivered the inhabitants of the land into my hands; and the land is subdued before the Lord and his people. [19]Now set your mind and heart to seek the Lord your God. Arise and build the sanctuary of the Lord God, so that the ark of the covenant of the Lord and the holy vessels of God may be brought into a house built for the name of the Lord."

With the purchase of the threshing floor of Ornan the Jebusite, the stage is set for the building of the Temple. It only remains in these last chapters to outline the further provisions for the Temple which the Chronicler implies were made by David before his death. First of all, some of the material provisions are listed but the remainder of the chapter deals with the more important matter of commissioning Solomon to undertake the task. It is interesting to compare the Chronicler's account with that of 1 Kings (2:1-9) where the son is asked to settle a few of the father's old scores. No such mundane preoccupation for the Chronicler; Solomon's concern is to be solely for the Temple and the "keeping of the law of the Lord your God" (v.12).

The reason why David himself could not build the Temple is at last made clear; he was a man of blood and underlying the text may be a strong psychological reaction against the shedding of blood. But Solomon, as his name signified, was a man of peace and so could safely undertake the program. Recent studies in this section of Chronicles imply that the author modelled the transition from the rule of David to Solomon on that from Moses to Joshua. Just as Moses was disqualified from leading the people into the Promised Land, so David was precluded from building the Temple. There is the same kind of commissioning the older of the younger, both in private (Deut 31:23; 1 Chron 22:6) and in the sight of all the people (Deut 31:7; 1 Chron 28:8). Both Joshua and Solomon are encouraged by the older men to "be strong and of good courage." A spirit of wisdom and understanding is given to them to accomplish their tasks with the assurance that God would be with them.

The purpose of the Chronicler would seem to have been to wield into a unity the reigns of David and Solomon by stressing the complementary nature of their functions, just as the leadership of Moses and Joshua was complementary in an earlier age. If this is correct, we have here an example of the conscious literary activity of the Chronicler, modelling his work on earlier sources of the Bible which would already have formed a literary unit.

David's Appointments
23:1-2.

> **23** When David was old and full of days, he made Solomon his son king over Israel.
>
> ²David assembled all the leaders of Israel and the priests and the Levites.

The first two verses of chapter twenty-three indicate David's concern to leave affairs in order behind him. Solomon's appointment as king is mentioned first (no account being taken of the struggle for succession as it appears in 1 Kings). Next comes the organisation of political leaders and finally mention is made of cultic personnel. The following chapters (23—27) give details of the activities of these functionaries.

There is almost universal agreement among scholars that these chapters are additions to the book of 1 Chronicles because of the fact that they interrupt the flow of the narrative which continues in 28:1 from 23:2 and because there is much overlapping of material within the chapters themselves and with other passages in the book. Even though these chapters are most likely additions, however, it has to be pointed out as well that whoever was responsible for their insertion into the book was consciously aiming at a definite organisation and arrangement of the material (see Intro. p. 9). The chapters take up the officials mentioned in 23:1-2 and give details of their function in reverse order from their positions in these verses: Temple functionaries are treated first (23:3-26:32) followed by the political leaders (27:1-34). The section is followed by the final portion of the book which deals with the public proclamation of Solomon as king.

Temple Functionaries
23:3—26:32.

a) The Levites
    23:3-32 (cf. 24:20-31)

> ³The Levites, thirty years old and upward, were numbered, and the total was thirty-eight thousand men. ⁴"Twenty-four thousand of these," David said, "shall have charge of the work in the house of the Lord, six thousand shall be officers and judges, ⁵four thousand gatekeepers, and four thousand shall offer praises to the Lord with the instruments which I have made for praise." ⁶And David organized them in divisions corresponding to the sons of Levi: Gershom, Kohath, and Merari....

24These were the sons of Levi by their fathers' houses,
the heads of fathers' houses as they were registered
according to the number of the names of the individuals
from twenty years old and upward who were to do the
work for the service of the house of the Lord. 25For David
said, "The Lord, the God of Israel, has given peace to his
people; and he dwells in Jerusalem for ever. 26And so the
Levites no longer need to carry the tabernacle or any of
the things for its service"—27for by the last words of
David these were the number of the Levites from twenty
years old and upward—28"but their duty shall be to assist
the sons of Aaron for the service of the house of the Lord,
having the care of the courts and the chambers, the
cleansing of all that is holy, and any work for the service
of the house of God; 29to assist also with the showbread,
the flour for the cereal offering, the wafers for unleavened
bread, the baked offering, the offering mixed with oil,
and all measures of quantity or size. 30And they shall
stand every morning, thanking and praising the Lord,
and likewise at evening, 31and whenever burnt offerings
are offered to the Lord on sabbaths, new moons, and
feast days, according to the number required of them,
continually before the Lord. 32Thus they shall keep
charge of the tent of meeting and the sanctuary, and shall
attend the sons of Aaron, their brethren, for the service of
the house of the Lord."

Details of the functions of Temple personnel, as was
pointed out in the Introduction (see p. 5, 6), owe more to
post-exilic times than to those of David. At the same time
they bear witness to the continuous insistence in the books
that if things are as they are in post-exilic times, it is because
the foundations for such a line of development were laid in
David's time. Two types of function are assigned to the
Levites in this chapter: in the first section they are seen as
overseers of Temple construction, musicians and gatekeepers in it when it would be built (these latter functions will be
treated separately). In the second section they are consid-

ered as assistants to the priests, preparing offerings and cleaning the Temple (23:28-32). This section would indicate the subordinate role of the Levites to the priests in cultic ceremonial (see Intro. p. 5) and it is possible that it is an example of an addition to the text from a source favourable to the priests.

The number of the Levites mentioned in the text are far and away beyond what would be realistic either in David's time or in that of the post-exilic Temple (cf. 1 Chron 12:23-37). The proportions of the numbers are interesting, however, in that the number assigned "work in the house of the Lord" is four times that of those who were to be "officers and judges" and six times those of the gatekeepers and musicians. This may also indicate an effort on the part of an editor to keep the Levites "in their place."

A discrepancy about the age for service also exists in this chapter; this is an indication that the sources used in the chapter are varied. In 23:3 the age is to be "thirty years old and upwards" while in 23:24 it is "twenty years old and upwards." This reflects a like discrepancy in other biblical books where the age is variously described as *thirty* (Num 4:3); *twenty-five* (Num 8:24); or *twenty* (Ezra 3:8).

b) The Priests
    24:1-19

24 The divisions of the sons of Aaron were these. The sons of Aaron: Nadam, Abihu, Eleazar, and Ithamar. ²But Nadab and Abihu died before their father, and had no children, so Eleazar and Ithamar became the priests. ³With the help of Zadok of the sons of Eleazar, and Ahimelech of the sons of Ithamar, David organized them according to the appointed duties in their service. ⁴Since more chief men were found among the sons of Eleazar than among the sons of Ithamar, they organized them under sixteen heads of fathers' houses of the sons of Eleazar, and eight of the sons of Ithamar. ⁵They organized them by lot, all alike, for there were officers of the sanctuary and officers of God among both the sons of Eleazar and the sons of Ithamar. ⁶And the scribe Shemaiah the son of Nethanel, a Levite, recorded them in the presence of the king, and the princes, and Zadok the priest, and Ahimelech the son of Abiathar, and the heads of the fathers' houses of the priests and of the Levites; one father's house being chosen for Eleazar and one chosen for Ithamar.

[7]The first lot fell to Jehoiarib, the second to Jedaiah, [8]the third to Harim, the fourth to Se-orim, [9]the fifth to Malchijah, the sixth to Mijamin, [10]the seventh to Hakkoz, the eighth to Abijah, [11]the ninth to Jeshua, the tenth to Shecaniah, [12]the eleventh to Eliashib, the twelfth to Jakim, [13]the thirteenth to Huppah, the fourteenth to Jeshebeab, [14]the fifteenth to Bilgah, the sixteenth to Immer, [15]the seventeenth to Hezir, the eighteenth to Happizzez, [16]the nineteenth to Pethahiah, the twentieth to Jehezkel, [17]the twenty-first to Jachin, the twenty-second to Gamul, [18]the twenty-third to Delaiah, the twenty-fourth to Maaziah. [19]These had as their appointed duty in their service to come into the house of the Lord according to the procedure established for them by Aaron their father, as the Lord God of Israel had commanded him.

Priesthood in Israel, as among many ancient peoples, was hereditary. Priests traditionally traced their ancestors back to Aaron, the brother of Moses (see Intro. p. 5). Of the four sons of Aaron, two dies childless; the fact that their death was considered a punishment for sin is not mentioned in Chronicles (cf. Num 26:61). Descent is, therefore, traced through the other two sons, Eleazar and Ithamar. The line of Eleazar was far more to the fore throughout the monarchal period and this is reflected here by the fact that he receives a double share of inheritance which was the right of the first-born. The line of Eleazar was important because Zadok, the most famous priest from the time of Solomon, was supposed to be descended from him. The family line through Ithamar asserted itself in post-exilic times (cf. Ezra 8:2) and this is why it is stressed in Chronicles.

In this chapter, Zadok is portrayed as organising with

David the twenty-four divisions of the priests who would fulfill their duties in turn by casting lots. There is no evidence in pre-exilic texts for such an organisation; some occurrence in post-exilic times must have given rise to the arrangement. It lasted as long as the Jewish priesthood itself functioned and is mentioned in the beginning of Luke's gospel: "In the days of Herod, king of Judea, there was a priest named Zechariah, of the division of Abijah..." (Lk 1:5; cf. 1 Chron 24:10).

There is some confusion about the name of the other priest who was said to have assisted David and Zadok. In this passage he is called Ahimelech (cf. 18:16), but elsewhere in Chronicles (e.g. 15:11), it is a priest called Abiathar who is associated with Zadok, while in 1 Sam 22:20, Abiathar is spoken of as one of the sons of Ahimelech. It is possible that the author did not wish the name of Abiathar associated with the priesthood in the account of the foundation of the Temple because he was the priest who sided with one of David's other sons, Adonijah, in trying to secure the kingship in place of Solomon (cf. 1 Kings 2).

c) The Musicians
   25:1-31

> **25** David and the chiefs of the service also set apart for the service certain of the sons of Asaph, and of Heman, and of Jeduthun, who should prophesy with lyres, with harps, and with cymbals. The list of those who did the work and of their duties was: ²Of the sons of Asaph: Zaccur, Joseph, Nethaniah, and Asharelah, sons of Asaph, under the direction of Asaph, who prophesied under the direction of the king. ³Of Jeduthun, the sons of Jeduthun: Gedaliah, Zeri, Jeshaiah, Shimei, Hashabiah, and Mattithiah, six, under the direction of their father Jeduthun, who prophesied with the lyre in thanksgiving and praise to the Lord. ⁴Of Heman, the sons of Heman: Bukkiah, Mattaniah, Uzziel, Shebuel, and Jerimoth, Hananiah, Hanani, Eliathah, Giddalti, and Romamtiezer, Joshbekashah, Mallothi, Hothir, Mahazioth. ⁵All these were the sons of Heman the king's

> seer, according to the promise of God to exalt him; for
> God had given Heman fourteen sons and three daughters.
> [6]They were all under the direction of their father in the
> music in the house of the Lord with cymbals, harps, and
> lyres for the service of the house of God. Asaph, Jedu-
> thun, and Heman were under the order of the king. [7]The
> number of them along with their brethren, who were
> trained in singing to the Lord, all who were skillful, was
> two hundred and eighty-eight. [8]And they cast lots for
> their duties, small and great, teacher and pupil alike.

The insistence that the musicians were to be considered as
Levites has appeared often already in the text (e.g. 1 Chron
15—16). The three chief musical families are again mentioned here (cf. 1 Chron 6:31-47) but prominence is given to
the family line of Heman whereas in 1 Chron 16 it was
Asaph alone who was mentioned. It is likely that different
family lines came into prominence at different stages of
post-exilic times and that the discrepancies in the lists may
again reflect editorial work (see p. 57).

The musicians are organised for Temple service here in
much the same way as priests and Levites: twenty-four
courses of two weeks each to ensure that the Temple would
never be left without service. One can visualise the great
schema of the author of these passages: Levites busy preparing the sacrifices, priests busy offering them and singers
and musicians praising with might and main the God to
whom the sacrifices were offered.

Music was not to be seen as mere decoration in the
Liturgy. In its own way it was just as important as sacrifice.
This point is made by speaking of the singers as "prophesying" (see Intro. p. 5, 6). The song was the voiced word and as
such it had power to inspire, to provoke to action like the
prophetic word of pre-exilic times. This was an insight
which gave its true place to liturgy in the awakening and
guiding of God's people. Unfortunately the instrumental
word is more liable to become a mere performance than the
urgent and vibrant word of the lone preacher. But certainly

in the vision of post-exilic circles, this was not how things should be.

d) The Gatekeepers and Other Officials
26:1-32

26 As for the divisions of the gatekeepers: of the Korahites, Meshelemiah the son of Kore, of the sons of Asaph. [2]And Meshelemiah had sons: Zechariah the first-born, Jediael the second, Zebadiah the third, Jathniel the fourth, [3]Elam the fifth, Jehohanan the sixth, Eliehoenai the seventh....

[12]These divisions of the gatekeepers, corresponding to their chief men, had duties, just as their brethren did, ministering in the house of the Lord; [13]and they cast lots by fathers' houses, small and great alike, for their gates. [14]The lot for the east fell to Shelemiah. They cast lots also for his son Zechariah, a shrewd counselor, and his lot came out for the north. [15]Obededom's came out for the south, and to his sons was allotted the storehouse. [16]For Shuppim and Hosah it came out for the west, at the gate of Shallecheth on the road that goes up. Watch corresponded to watch. [17]On the east there were six each day, on the north four each day, on the south four each day, as well as two and two at the storehouse; [18]and for the parbar on the west there were four at the road and two at the parbar. [19]These were the divisions of the gatekeepers among the Korahites and the sons of Merari....

[22]The sons of Jehieli, Zetham and Joel his brother, were in charge of the treasuries of the house of the Lord. [23]Of the Amramites, the Izharites, the Hebronites, and the Uzzielites—[24]and Shebuel the son of Gershom, son of Moses, was chief officer in charge of the treasuries. [25]His brethren: from Eliezer were his son Rehabiah, and his son Jeshaiah, and his son Joram, and his son Zichri, and his son Shelomoth. [26]This Shelomoth and his brethren were in charge of all the treasuries of the dedicated gifts which David the king, and the heads of the fathers' houses, and the officers of the thousands and the hundreds, and the commanders of the army, had dedicated. [27]From spoil

won in battles they dedicated gifts for the maintenance of the house of the Lord. [28]Also all that Samuel the seer, and Saul the son of Kish, and Abner the son of Ner, and Joab the son of Zeruiah had dedicated—all dedicated gifts were in the care of Shelomoth and his brethren.

[29]Of the Izharites, Chenaniah and his sons were appointed to outside duties for Israel, as officers and judges. [30]Of the Hebronites, Hashabiah and his brethren, one thousand seven hundred men of ability, had the oversight of Israel westward of the Jordan for all the work of the Lord and for the service of the king. [31]Of the Hebronites, Jerijah was chief of the Hebronites of whatever genealogy or fathers' houses. (In the fortieth year of David's reign search was made and men of great ability among them were found at Jazer in Gilead.) [32]King David appointed him and his brethren, two thousand seven hundred men of ability, heads of fathers' houses, to have the oversight of the Reubenites, the Gadites, and the half-tribe of the Manassites for everything pertaining to God and for the affairs of the king.

The Levites were earlier connected in Chronicles with warfare and defence by being included in the list of armed troups who came to David at Hebron (1 Chron 12:26). The gatekeepers of post-exilic times are here transferred back to the first Temple. Security personnel have always been a necessity for big buildings and the Temple was no exception. This chapter gives the gatekeepers levitical status (cf. 1 Chron 9:17-27), considering that they performed a vital function in the cult. This was not merely in the realm of security; the psalms bear witness to the function of the gatekeepers in the actual cult itself where in a solemn procession to the Temple they would perform the ceremonial opening of the gates. Psalm 24 [23] for instance says: "Lift up your heads, O gates: and be lifted up, O ancient door: that the King of glory may come in."

The gates mentioned in the text here are more likely to have been those of post-exilic times, for example it is likely that there was no gate to the south in Solomon's Temple since the palace adjoined the Temple area at that point (cf. Ezek 40:24). The *parbar* mentioned in 26:18 was probably a court or colonade which needed particular attention. Security was also necessary for the treasuries and those in charge are detailed in vv.20-28 (cf. 1 Chron 9:28-29). The dedicated gifts come from all sections of the people: kings, seers, generals. This emphasises the central place the Temple was to occupy in the life of the people.

The last section of chapter twenty-six describes the levitical functionaries who performed tasks among the people rather than in relation to the Temple itself. If these functions were for the collection of taxes the account would follow naturally from 26:20-28. Some type of judicial function seems to be envisaged for them, however, and this would tally with the growing importance of the Levites in the community for the regulation of affairs of the people other than those of the cult (cf. Neh 11:16).

Political and Military Organisation
27:1-32.

27 This is the list of the people of Israel, the heads of fathers' houses, the commanders of thousands and hundreds, and their officers who served the king in all matters concerning the divisions that came and went, month after month throughout the year, each division numbering twenty-four thousand:

²Jashobeam the son of Zabdiel was in charge of the first division in the first month; in his division were twenty-four thousand....

¹⁶Over the tribes of Israel, for the Reubenites Eliezer the son of Zichri was chief officer; for the Simeonites, Shephatiah the son of Maacah; ¹⁷for Levi, Hashabiah the son of Kemuel; for Aaron, Zadok; ¹⁸for Judah, Elihu, one of David's brothers; for Issachar, Omri the son of Michael; ¹⁹for Zebulun, Ishmaiah the son of Obadiah; for Naphtali, Jeremoth the son of Azriel; ²⁰for the Ephraimites, Hoshea the son of Azaziah; for the half-tribe of

Manasseh, Joel the son of Pedaiah; 21for the half-tribe of
Manasseh in Gilead, Iddo the son of Zechariah; for Benjamin, Jaasiel the son of Abner; 22for Dan, Azarel the son
of Jeroham. These were the leaders of the tribes of Israel.
25Over the king's treasuries was Azmaveth the son of
Adiel; and over the treasuries in the country, in the cities,
in the villages and in the towers, was Jonathan the son of
Uzziah; 26and over those who did the work in the field
for tilling the soil was Ezri the son of Chelub; 27and over
the vineyards was Shimei the Ramathite; and over the
produce of the vineyards for the wine cellars was Zabdi
the Shiphmite. 28Over the olive and sycamore trees in
the Shephelah was Baalhanan the Gederite; and over the
stores of oil was Joash. 29Over the herds that pastured
in Sharon was Shitrai the Sharonite; over the herds in
the valleys was Shaphat the son of Adlai. 30Over the
camels was Obil the Ishmaelite; and over the she-asses
was Jehdeiah the Meronothite. Over the flocks was Jaziz
the Hagrite. 31All these were stewards of King David's
property.

The list of divisional commanders corresponds closely
to the list of David's mighty men in chapter eleven. The
precise organisation into units with numerals of twelve is
too detailed for David's time. The Chronicler loved having
his lists based on numerals of twelve (cf. 1 Chron 24:7-19;
Ezra 8:24), possibly because of the sense of completeness it
gave. Based on the division of the year into twelve months it
is still today used as a round number, for example in the
make-up of a jury. It was always a sacred number in Israel,
going back to the time of the twelve tribes whom the Chronicler enumerates here alongside the later military divisions.
The reason for twelve tribes originally may have been due to
the necessity of providing service at the central shrine each
month in rotation. The actual names in the composition of
the tribes have always been fluid; here the Chronicler omits
Gad and Asher and makes up the twelve by counting the two
half tribes of Manasseh and including Simeon as a tribe,

even though Simeon had long ago been commuted with Judah as its territory had been absorbed into that of Judah long before the time of David.

Next follows the account of the men appointed as overseers of David's possessions. This is near enough to the historical situation of a David who would have lived off the property he acquired in warfare rather than from the taxes levied on his people. At the same time there is some discrepancy with other sections of Chronicles where David is said to have dedicated all war booty to the Temple (cf. 26:26).

David's Counselors
27:32-34

32Jonathan, David's uncle, was a counselor, being a man of understanding and a scribe; he and Jehiel the son of Hachmoni attended the king's sons. 33Ahithophel was the king's counselor, and Hushai the Archite was the king's friend. 34Ahithophel was succeeded by Jehoiada the son of Benaiah, and Abiathar. Joab was commander of the king's army.

There is no mention of an uncle of David who was a counselor of his elsewhere in the tradition. Since the word for *uncle* in Hebrew could also be translated *beloved,* it is conjectured that Jonathan, the son of Saul and the beloved friend of David, may be underlying the text here. As his beloved friend there is a real sense in which Jonathan could be considered David's first counselor (cf. 1 Sam 20). That friend can also mean close adviser is clear from Egyptian documents; in verse thirty-three, Hushai is called the king's friend and this clearly means his counselor since he was the one who stood by David at the time of Absolom's revolt (cf. 2 Sam 17). Ahithophel was the counselor who betrayed David at this time by going over to Absolom. We are meant to know about this episode from the earlier histories because the Chronicler goes on to mention the fact that Ahithophel was succeeded in office by Jehoida, the son of Benaiah, and by Abiathar. This is possibly the same Abia-

thar who was a priest at the time of David but we saw earlier
the reasons why the Chronicler scrupled to give him the title
priest. Instead he is listed as a counselor. The military man,
Joab, completes the list.

David's Instructions Concerning the Temple
28:1-21

28   David assembled at Jerusalem all the officials of
Israel, the officials of the tribes, the officers of the divisions that served the king, the commanders of thousands, the commanders of hundreds, the stewards of all
the property and cattle of the king and his sons, together
with the palace officials, the mighty men, and all the
seasoned warriors. ²Then King David rose to his feet and
said: "Hear me, my brethren and my people. I had it in
my heart to build a house of rest for the ark of the
covenant of the Lord, and for the footstool of our God;
and I made preparations for building. ³But God said to
me, 'You may not build a house for my name, for you are
a warrior and have shed blood.' ⁴Yet the Lord God of
Israel chose me from all my father's house to be king over
Israel for ever; for he chose Judah as leader, and in the
house of Judah my father's house, and among my father's
sons he took pleasure in me to make me king over all
Israel. ⁵And of all my sons (for the Lord has given me
many sons) he has chosen Solomon my son to sit upon
the throne of the kingdom of the Lord over Israel. ⁶He
said to me, 'It is Solomon your son who shall build my
house and my courts, for I have chosen him to be my son,
and I will be his father. ⁷I will establish his kingdom for
ever if he continues resolute in keeping my commandments and my ordinances, as he is today.' ⁸Now therefore
in the sight of all Israel, the assembly of the Lord, and in
the hearing of our God, observe and seek out all the
commandments of the Lord your God; that you may
possess this good land, and leave it for an inheritance to
your children after you for ever.

⁹"And you, Solomon my son, know the God of your

father, and serve him with a whole heart and with a willing mind; for the Lord searches all hearts, and understands every plan and thought. If you seek him, he will be found by you; but if you forsake him, he will cast you off for ever. [10]Take heed now, for the Lord has chosen you to build a house for the sanctuary; be strong, and do it."

[11]Then David gave Solomon his son the plan of the vestibule of the temple, and of its houses, its treasuries, its upper rooms, and its inner chambers, and of the room for the mercy seat; [12]and the plan of all that he had in mind for the courts of the house of the Lord, all the surrounding chambers, the treasuries of the house of God, and the treasuries for dedicated gifts; [13]for the divisions of the priests and of the Levites, and all the work of the service in the house of the Lord; for all the vessels for the service in the house of the Lord. . . .

[20]Then David said to Solomon his son, "Be strong and of good courage, and do it. Fear not, be not dismayed; for the Lord God, even my God, is with you. He will not fail you or forsake you, until all the work for the service of the house of the Lord is finished. [21]And behold the divisions of the priests and the Levites for all the service of the house of God; and with you in all the work will be every willing man who has skill for any kind of service; also the officers and all the people will be wholly at your command."

Chapter 28:1 takes up from 23:2 (see p. 56) and presents us with a grand assembly of all the leaders of Israel gathered to assist at the coronation of Solomon as David's successor. The succession takes place because of God's choice and not through heredity, as David points out in his speech for the occasion. It was not because he was the first-born that David himself had become king, but because of God's choice and so likewise with Solomon. The Chronicler again bypasses completely the domestic quarrels over the succession. For him there is a serene passing on of authority from David to Solomon in the presence of all the state's officials, including the remainder of the king's sons.

But the interest in the chapter is not in the passing on of the powers of government to Solomon, as might be expected, but in the handing on of instructions concerning the building of the Temple — down to a detailed plan for its completion. That this plan was not an architect's line drawing, is clear from verse nineteen where it is spoken of as a "writing from the hand of the Lord." It is possible that the Chronicler is consciously modelling himself here on the plan for the tabernacle reputedly given by God to Moses in the desert (cf. Ex 25:9).

The words with which David began his address to the people are a good indication of how kingship was considered in Israel: "Hear me my brethren and my people...." Essentially the king is no more than a brother of the rest of God's people and his election is for their sake (1 Chron 14:2). Through him God will govern the people. In this sense he will be in a special relationship to God himself and can call him "Father" (cf. v.6; Ps 2).

The tone of this speech has much in common with the type of writing contained in the Book of Deuteronomy and in some of the prophets. It is a type of preaching which is hortatory in character, insisting on the need to serve God with a "whole heart" (cf. Deut 6:5; Jer 24:7) and to seek him in such a way that he may be found (cf. Deut 4:29; Jer 29:13). There are many such speeches in 2 Chronicles; they are often spoken of as "levitical sermons" since they illustrate the kind of teaching engaged in by the Levites in the post-exilic period (cf. 2 Chron 13:4-12; 16:7-9). They do not give original prophecies themselves but, put on the lips of kings or prophets, they make actual for a later time insights contained in the earlier writings (e.g. 2 Chron 15:2-7; see Intro. p. 3, 6).

The sermons are inserted at suitable moments in the text, either at the climax of events as in this chapter or, more often, at decisive turning-points in the narrative (e.g. 2 Chron 13:4-12; 20:15-17). The first part of the sermon could be doctrinal in character, giving the reasons why God should come to the people's help (vv.2-3; cf. vv.6-7); the second often illustrated this from the past (vv.4-5), while the third part was usually an exhortation to follow God's ways in the present situation (vv.8-10). Sermons such as these were probably delivered by levitical teachers sent around the country to teach the people (cf. 2 Chron 30:6-10; Neh 8). It is possible also that such sermons were written down and available to the Chronicler (cf. 2 Chron 21:12-15). Adapted to their contexts, they were a powerful means of forwarding the Chronicler's theology at given points of the text.

Offerings for the Temple and David's Thanksgiving
29:1-19

29 And David the king said to all the assembly, "Solomon my son, whom alone God has chosen, is young and inexperienced, and the work is great; for the palace will not be for man but for the Lord God. ²So I have provided for the house of my God, so far as I was able, the gold for the things of gold, the silver for the things of silver, and the bronze for the things of bronze.. . .

⁶Then the heads of fathers' houses made their freewill offerings, as did also the leaders of the tribes, the commanders of thousands and of hundreds, and the officers over the king's work. ⁷They gave for the service of the house of God five thousand talents and ten thousand darics of gold, ten thousand talents of silver, eighteen thousand talents of bronze, and a hundred thousand talents of iron. ⁸And whoever had precious stones gave them to the treasury of the house of the Lord, in the care of Jehiel the Gershonite. ⁹Then the people rejoiced because these had given willingly, for with a whole heart they had offered freely to the Lord; David the king also rejoiced greatly.

¹⁰Therefore David blessed the Lord in the presence of all the assembly; and David said: "Blessed art thou, O Lord, the God of Israel our father, for ever and ever. ¹¹Thine, O Lord, is the greatness, and the power, and the glory, and the victory, and the majesty; for all that is in

the heavens and in the earth is thine; thine is the kingdom, O Lord, and thou art exalted as head above all. [12]Both riches and honor come from thee, and thou rulest over all. In thy hand are power and might; and in thy hand it is to make great and to give strength to all. [13]And now we thank thee, our God, and praise thy glorious name.

[14]"But who am I, and what is my people, that we should be able thus to offer willingly? For all things come from thee, and of thy own have we given thee. [15]For we are strangers before thee, and sojourners, as all our fathers were; our days on the earth are like a shadow, and there is no abiding. [16]O Lord our God, all this abundance that we have provided for building thee a house for thy holy name comes from thy hand and is all thy own. [17]I know, my God, that thou triest the heart, and hast pleasure in uprightness; in the uprightness of my heart I have freely offered all these things, and now I have seen thy people, who are present here, offering freely and joyously to thee. [18]O Lord, the God of Abraham, Isaac, and Israel, our fathers, keep for ever such purposes and thoughts in the hearts of thy people, and direct their hearts toward thee. [19]Grant to Solomon my son that with a whole heart he may keep thy commandments, thy testimonies, and thy statutes, performing all, and that he may build the palace for which I have made provision."

Those of us who have ever engaged in the heartbreaks of fund raising drives for Church expenses will envy David his ability here to get his officials to open their purse strings so freely. True he is portrayed as setting the example himself and feels free to ask on the principle that "God loves a cheerful giver" (2 Cor 9:7). The Chronicler, of course, has one eye on the people of his own time in his portrayal of the generosity of former times. For him the spontaneous gift of oneself and of one's possessions to God was to be part of the new covenant and again it is to be done with a "whole heart" (v.9; cf. 28:9). David sees this as only giving back to God what God has already given to him.

For all that he had received, the Chronicler has David give thanks in a thanksgiving prayer, the form of which can be found elsewhere in the Bible (cf. Gen 24:27; Dan 2:20-23; Tob 8:5-7). This is one of the most beautiful of these thanksgiving prayers and probably the best known passage in the books of Chronicles. It is an expression of wonder at the power of God and of joy in the fact that this power has been used by him on behalf of his people. The present graciousness of God is situated within the context of Abraham, Isaac and Jacob and of God's covenant with them. David prays that his people's hearts will be directed wholly towards God and in particular that Solomon his son will serve God with a "whole heart."

Final Acts of David
29:20-30

²⁰Then David said to all the assembly, "Bless the Lord your God." And all the assembly blessed the Lord, the God of their fathers, and bowed their heads, and worshiped the Lord, and did obeisance to the king. ²¹And they performed sacrifices to the Lord, and on the next day offered burnt offerings to the Lord, a thousand bulls, a thousand rams, and a thousand lambs, with their drink offerings, and sacrifices in abundance for all Israel; ²²and they ate and drank before the Lord on that day with great gladness.

And they made Solomon the son of David king the second time, and they anointed him as prince for the Lord, and Zadok as priest. ²³Then Solomon sat on the throne of the Lord as king instead of David his father; and he prospered, and all Israel obeyed him. ²⁴All the leaders and the mighty men, and also all the sons of King David, pledged their allegiance to King Solomon. ²⁵And the Lord gave Solomon great repute in the sight of all Israel, and bestowed upon him such royal majesty as had not been on any king before him in Israel.

²⁶Thus David the son of Jesse reigned over all Israel. ²⁷The time that he reigned over Israel was forty years; he

reigned seven years in Hebron, and thirty-three years in Jerusalem. [28]Then he died in a good old age, full of days, riches, and honor; and Solomon his son reigned in his stead. [29]Now the acts of King David, from first to last, are written in the Chronicles of Samuel the seer, and in the Chronicles of Nathan the prophet, and in the Chronicles of Gad the seer, [30]with accounts of all his rule and his might and of the circumstances that came upon him and upon Israel, and upon all the kingdoms of the countries.

The ritual of Solomon's commissioning to build the Temple is completed with solemn blessings, sacrifices and a feast. This pattern will be repeated when the Temple is completed (2 Chron 5). Solomon is publicly proclaimed king and David is allowed to retire from the stage "full of days, riches and honour" but without any mention of the dotage which seems to have marred his last days and which nearly cost Solomon the kingship (1 Kings 1, 2).

1 Chronicles ends with a notice of the sources which the Chronicler purported to use for his material. Much speculation has arisen as to whether there ever was a "Chronicle of Samuel the seer" and a "Chronicle of Nathan the prophet" and "the Chronicle of Gad the seer." The consensus among scholars seems to be that the main source used is 1 and 2 Samuel, since whenever the Chronicler mentions these prophets he is merely using material presented about them in the earlier histories.

III. SOLOMON, BUILDER OF THE TEMPLE
2 Chron 1:1—9:31.

There is no real break between the end of the first book of Chronicles and the beginning of the second; the reign of Solomon is a continuation of that of David. Solomon completes the work of David, in particular by building the Temple. That this is the central concern of the Chronicler can be judged from the fact that six of the nine chapters alloted to Solomon are devoted to it. Other aspects of his reign receive less attention. His proverbial wisdom, for instance, is not as much stressed as in Kings, the famous story of the harlots' babies being omitted altogether as is the notice about his encyclopaedic knowledge (1 Kings 3:16-28; 4:29-34). The weak points of Solomon's reign are also, characteristically, omitted such as the struggles with which it began and the sins with which it ended. On the whole, however, the description of Solomon's reign (and indeed the whole of 2 Chronicles) follows more closely its source in Kings than does the description of David's reign. Additions chiefly concern the cult and the Temple, for example the functions of the Levites are spelt out in great detail (compare 5:11-13 with 1 Kings 8:10-11).

THE BLESSINGS GIVEN TO SOLOMON
1:1-17.

1   Solomon the son of David established himself in his kingdom, and the Lord his God was with him and made him exceedingly great.

²Solomon spoke to all Israel, to the commanders of thousands and of hundreds, to the judges, and to all the leaders in all Israel, the heads of fathers' houses. ³And Solomon, and all the assembly with him, went to the high place that was at Gibeon, for the tent of meeting of God, which Moses the servant of the Lord had made in the wilderness, was there. ⁴(But David had brought up the ark of God from Kiriathjearim to the place that David had prepared for it, for he had pitched a tent for it in Jerusalem.) ⁵Moreover the bronze altar that Bezalel the son of Uri, son of Hur, had made, was there before the tabernacle of the Lord. And Solomon and the assembly sought the Lord. ⁶And Solomon went up there to the bronze altar before the Lord, which was at the tent of meeting, and offered a thousand burnt offerings upon it.

⁷In that night God appeared to Solomon, and said to him, "Ask what I shall give you." ⁸And Solomon said to God, "Thou hast shown great and steadfast love to David my father, and hast made me king in his stead. ⁹O Lord God, let thy promise to David my father be now fulfilled, for thou hast made me king over a people as many as the dust of the earth. ¹⁰Give me now wisdom and knowledge to go out and come in before this people, for who can rule this thy people, that is so great?" ¹¹God answered Solomon, "Because this was in your heart, and you have not asked possessions, wealth, honor, or the life of those who hate you, and have not even asked long life, but have asked wisdom and knowledge for yourself that you may rule my people over whom I have made you king, ¹²wisdom and knowledge are granted to you. I will also give you riches, possessions, and honor, such as none of the kings had who were before you, and none after you shall have the like.". . .

¹⁴Solomon gathered together chariots and horsemen; he had fourteen hundred chariots and twelve thousand horsemen, whom he stationed in the chariot cities and with the king in Jerusalem. ¹⁵And the king made silver and gold as common in Jerusalem as stone, and he made cedar as plentiful as the sycamore of the Shephelah. ¹⁶And Solomon's import of horses was from Egypt and Kue, and the king's traders received them from Kue for a price. ¹⁷They imported a chariot from Egypt for six hundred shekels of silver, and a horse for a hundred and fifty; likewise through them these were exported to all the kings of the Hittites and the kings of Syria.

"All Israel" is again present for the first great act of Solomon's reign: an offering to the Lord at Gibeon. Gibeon had once been the greatest shrine in Israel; now it is but a stage on the way to Jerusalem. The Chronicler legitimises Solomon's going there by linking the place to the tent of meeting and the bronze altar of the desert period (Ex 27:1-2). The account of the dialogue between God and Solomon which takes place on Gebron has been skillfully condensed from Kings (cf. 1 Kings 3:5-14). The blessings promised by God — wisdom, wealth and power — are those which would enable him to rule well. In later Jewish thinking they came to be regarded as a sign of God's favour.

What was probably Solomon's chief occupation is dismissed in a few verses (1:14-17); this was to act as a middleman in the lucrative trade between Egypt to the South and Syria and other countries to the North. Israel's position as a narrow strip of land between the Mediterranean coast and the Arabian desert has always provided a source of income in trade in times of peace. Unfortunately it seldom enjoyed peace as this very position prompted rapacious neighbours to grasp control of the trade routes. At least during the time of Solomon, this position was exploited to the full.

Many of the cities built or enlarged by Solomon, such as Hazor, Megiddo, and Bethshan, have been excavated and remains of store houses and of what could have been stables for his horses have been unearthed. The archeological remains bear witness to the sharp increase of wealth in the land at this time; pottery and buildings reached a new perfection and many imported items were found but the cost of Solomon's rash building programs had yet to be reckoned.

ERECTING THE TEMPLE
2:1—7:22.

Preparations
2:1-18.

2 Now Solomon purposed to build a temple for the name of the Lord, and a royal palace for himself. ²And Solomon assigned seventy thousand men to bear burdens and eighty thousand to quarry in the hill country, and three thousand six hundred to oversee them. ³And Solomon sent word to Huram the king of Tyre: "As you dealt with David my father and sent him cedar to build himself a house to dwell in, so deal with me. ⁴Behold, I am about to build a house for the name of the Lord my God and dedicate it to him for the burning of incense of sweet spices before him, and for the continual offering of the showbread, and for burnt offerings morning and evening, on the sabbaths and the new moons and the appointed feasts of the Lord our God, as ordained for ever for Israel. ⁵The house which I am to build will be great, for our God is greater than all gods. ⁶But who is able to build him a house, since heaven, even highest heaven, cannot contain him? Who am I to build a house for him, except as a place to burn incense before him? ⁷So now send me a man skilled to work in gold, silver, bronze, and iron, and in purple, crimson, and blue fabrics, trained also in engraving, to be with the skilled workers who are with me in Judah and Jerusalem, whom David my father provided. ⁸Send me also cedar, cypress, and algum timber from

Lebanon, for I know that your servants know how to cut
timber in Lebanon. And my servants will be with your
servants, [9]to prepare timber for me in abundance, for the
house I am to build will be great and wonderful. [10]I will
give for your servants, the hewers who cut timber, twenty
thousand cors of crushed wheat, twenty thousand cors of
barley, twenty thousand baths of wine, and twenty thousand baths of oil."

Solomon at last sets about the task of building the Temple. But Temple building on a grand scale was not something Israelites knew much about, so the enlisting of foreign
aid was imperative. This was obtained from the old ally of
David, Huram of Tyre, who provides the finest building
materials and sent a craftsman to supervise the work. The
Phoenician character of the Temple was, as a result, quite
marked.

The purpose which the Temple would serve is described in
Solomon's letter to Huram. The Chronicler has inserted
into his source here an addition from a later passage of
Kings (cf. 1 Kings 8:27). Earlier times may have considered
the Temple as a place where God has his dwelling among the
people and where his presence would be realised. But the
Chronicler is careful to point out that God cannot be confined to a building. This was a lesson which was continually
being hammered home by the prophets (cf. Jer 7; Ezek 2)
and which was at last realised in Exile. The Temple was not
to be a house for God but a place where his people could
pray to him and offer sacrifice. This was the function of the
liturgy carried on in the Temple. The liturgy was never an
end in itself, merely a beautiful performance or the correct
carrying out of ritual, though it could often degenerate into
that. Its purpose was to recall past favours of God to his
people so that they would be reminded in the present of the
kind of God with whom they were in relation. He is a God
who had been a Saviour in the past, is with them now and
will be for the future. For the Chronicler, therefore, it was in
the Temple liturgy, duly performed by the correct person-

nel, that the meeting between God and his people took place.

Place and Plan of the Temple
3:1—5:1.

3 Then Solomon began to build the house of the Lord in Jerusalem on Mount Moriah, where the Lord had appeared to David his father, at the place that David had appointed, on the threshing floor of Ornan the Jebusite. ²He began to build in the second month of the fourth year of his reign. ³These are Solomon's measurements for building the house of God: the length, in cubits of the old standard, was sixty cubits, and the breadth twenty cubits. ⁴The vestibule in front of the nave of the house was twenty cubits long, equal to the width of the house; and its height was a hundred and twenty cubits. He overlaid it on the inside with pure gold. ⁵The nave he lined with cypress, and covered it with fine gold, and made palms and chains on it. ⁶He adorned the house with settings of precious stones. The gold was gold of Parvaim. ⁷So he lined the house with gold—its beams, its thresholds, its walls, and its doors; and he carved cherubim on the walls.

⁸And he made the most holy place; its length, corresponding to the breadth of the house, was twenty cubits; and its breadth was twenty cubits; he overlaid it with six hundred talents of fine gold....

4 ¹⁹So Solomon made all the things that were in the house of God: the golden altar, the tables for the bread of the Presence, ²⁰the lampstands and their lamps of pure gold to burn before the inner sanctuary, as prescribed; ²¹the flowers, the lamps, and the tongs, of purest gold; ²²the snuffers, basins, dishes for incense, and firepans, of pure gold; and the sockets of the temple, for the inner doors to the most holy place and for the doors of the nave of the temple were of gold.

5 Thus all the work that Solomon did for the house of the Lord was finished. And Solomon brought in the things which David his father had dedicated, and stored the silver, the gold, and all the vessels in the treasuries of the house of God.

Both Chronicles and Kings deliberately link the foundation of Solomon's Temple with Israel's past but they do so in different ways. Kings links it to the Exodus (1 Kings 6:1), the great founding event of the people's history, and so insists that a new founding event has taken place with the building of the Temple. Chronicles, on the other hand, goes further back and links it with the Patriarch, Abraham, by saying that the Temple was built "in Jerusalem on Mount Moriah." Mount Moriah (cf. Is 30:29) was the mountain on which traditionally Abraham sacrificed Isaac (Gen 22:2). The link is made by means of the "threshing floor of Ornan the Jebusite" (see pp. 52-53). In the purchase of this site as detailed in 1 Chron 21, the parallel with Abraham was also clear (cf. Gen 23).

As Jerusalem became the spiritual home of Israelites, many of the traditions from their past found a way into its history. Mount Moriah was the place where Abraham came to know God in a new way, so in the Temple the people of Israel would have a new and definitive approach to their God.

Solomon began the actual building of the Temple four years after becoming king. It is very difficult to visualise what exactly the original Temple looked like, since the only descriptions we have of it come from the text here and other literary sources and the writers were not architects outlining precise plans. The diagram on the following page gives an artist's impression of what the plan of the original Temple might have been.

What can be ascertained from the above diagram is that the Temple was in the form of a long building with three divisions, one behind the other in a straight line, a vestibule in front, next the holy place which was the Temple proper and behind this again, the most holy place. This type of Temple building was common among Israel's neighbours, especially in the Syro-Phoenician region. It is more than

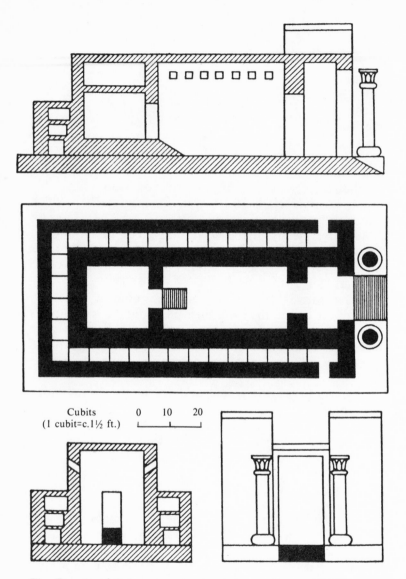

Cubits
(1 cubit=c.1½ ft.)   0   10   20

The Temple of Solomon, reconstructed according to Old Testament specifications and archaeological study.

likely that Solomon imported his architect from there as well as his chief craftsman. Even for the expression of its religious cult forms, Israel borrowed much from the peoples round about them. After completing the Temple, Solomon brings all the dedicated articles which David had set aside into the treasuries of the house of God (cf. 1 Chron 26:26).

The Dedication of the Temple
5:2—6:2.

²Then Solomon assembled the elders of Israel and all the heads of the tribes, the leaders of the fathers' houses of the people of Israel, in Jerusalem, to bring up the ark of the covenant of the Lord out of the city of David, which is Zion. ³And all the men of Israel assembled before the king at the feast which is in the seventh month. ⁴And all the elders of Israel came, and the Levites took up the ark. ⁵And they brought up the ark, the tent of meeting, and all the holy vessels that were in the tent; the priests and the Levites brought them up. ⁶And King Solomon and all the congregation of Israel, who had assembled before him, were before the ark, sacrificing so many sheep and oxen that they could not be counted or numbered. ⁷So the priests brought the ark of the covenant of the Lord to its place, in the inner sanctuary of the house. . . .
¹²And all the Levitical singers, Asaph, Heman, and Jeduthun, their sons and kinsmen, arrayed in fine linen, with cymbals, harps, and lyres, stood east of the altar with a hundred and twenty priests who were trumpeters; ¹³and it was the duty of the trumpeters and singers to make themselves heard in unison in praise and thanksgiving to the Lord), and when the song was raised, with trumpets and cymbals and other musical instruments, in praise to the Lord,

"For he is good,
for his steadfast love endures for ever,"

the house, the house of the Lord, was filled with a cloud, ¹⁴so that the priests could not stand to minister because of the cloud; for the glory of the Lord filled the house of God.

6   Then Solomon said,
    "The Lord has said that he would
    dwell in thick darkness.
²I have built thee an exalted house,
    a place for thee to dwell in for ever."

The Ark comes to its final resting place in the Temple, brought in solemn procession by Solomon and "all Israel" and carried, as the Chronicler is careful to point out, by the Levites. It is the priests, however, who place it in the innermost sanctuary, the most holy place. This is the signal for a great musical outburst culminating in the refrain of Ps 136 [135], a refrain which will often be repeated in subsequent chapters where there is mention of praise.

The filling of the Temple with the cloud, symbol of God's presence with his people, is a sign of God's acceptance of the house dedicated to him. The cloud was equated with the glory of God, the manifestation of God's power and might (cf. Ex 16:7; Num 14:22), a manifestation which is paradoxically veiled. This is further emphasised in the remark of Solomon: "the Lord has said that he will dwell in thick darkness," which refers either to the cloud or to the darkness of the inner room of the Temple. It is a fact of religious experience that it is only by entering into the darkness that one can perceive the light of God (cf. Ex 24:17-18; Sir 45:5).

Solomon's Prayer
6:3-42.

³Then the king faced about, and blessed all the assembly of Israel, while all the assembly of Israel stood. ⁴And he said, "Blessed be the Lord, the God of Israel, who with his hand has fulfilled what he promised with his mouth to David my father. . . .
¹⁸"But will God dwell indeed with man on the earth? Behold, heaven and the highest heaven cannot contain thee; how much less this house which I have built! ¹⁹Yet have regard to the prayer of thy servant and to his supplication, O Lord my God, hearkening to the cry and to the

prayer which thy servant prays before thee; [20]that thy eyes may be open day and night toward this house, the place where thou hast promised to set thy name, that thou mayest hearken to the prayer which thy servant offers toward this place. [21]And hearken thou to the supplications of thy servant and of thy people Israel, when they pray toward this place; yea, hear thou from heaven thy dwelling place; and when thou hearest, forgive.....

[36]"If they sin against thee—for there is no man who does not sin—and thou art angry with them, and dost give them to an enemy, so that they are carried away captive to a land far or near; [37]yet if they lay it to heart in the land to which they have been carried captive, and repent, and make supplication to thee in the land of their captivity, saying, 'We have sinned, and have acted perversely and wickedly'; [38]if they repent with all their mind and with all their heart in the land of their captivity, to which they were carried captive, and pray toward their land, which thou gavest to their fathers, the city which thou hast chosen, and the house which I have built for thy name, [39]then hear thou from heaven thy dwelling place their prayer and their supplications, and maintain their cause and forgive thy people who have sinned against thee. [40]Now, O my God, let thy eyes be open and thy ears attentive to a prayer of this place.

[41]"And now arise, O Lord God, and go to thy resting place,
  thou and the ark of thy might.
Let thy priests, O Lord God, be clothed with salvation,
  and let thy saints rejoice in thy goodness.
[42]O Lord God, do not turn away the face of thy anointed one!
Remember thy steadfast love for David thy servant."

The solemn dedicatory prayer of the Temple is spoken by Solomon. He first of all *blesses* God, a word which is best translated in our terms as thanksgiving. He thanks God for his choice of Jerusalem, his choice of David and, above all, his choice of himself to be the builder of the Temple. Then with hands outstretched he asks that God will always be turned favourably towards his people. Again there is the insistence that God cannot be confined to the Temple; instead it is the privileged place where the petitions of the people may be presented. The petitions listed in the chapter (of which only a sample have been printed here) are concerned with the happiness of all the people and not merely with that of the king alone. They include such practical matters as the need for rain, protection from enemies, famine, blight, sickness and the other afflictions which can plague a stricken people. This prayer of Solomon's is one of the best examples in the Bible of the importance of petition in prayer.

The ending of the prayer is different from that of Kings. Instead of the reference to Moses and the Exodus which is there, the Chronicler substitutes a psalm. It is a psalm of David, the implication being that the promises made to David find their initial fulfillment in the building of the Temple. This again points up the emphasis on the reign of David as a founding event.

Ratification of the Temple
7:1-22

7 When Solomon had ended his prayer, fire came down from heaven and consumed the burnt offering and the sacrifices, and the glory of the Lord filled the temple. . . .

[11]Thus Solomon finished the house of the Lord and the king's house; all that Solomon had planned to do in the house of the Lord and in his own house he successfully accomplished. [12]Then the Lord appeared to Solomon in the night and said to him: "I have heard your prayer, and have chosen this place for myself as a house of sacrifice. [13]When I shut up the heavens so that there is no rain, or command the locust to devour the land, or send pestilence among my people, [14]if my people who are called by

my name humble themselves, and pray and seek my face, and turn from their wicked ways, then I will hear from heaven, and will forgive their sin and heal their land. [15]Now my eyes will be open and my ears attentive to the prayer that is made in this place. [16]For now I have chosen and consecrated this house that my name may be there for ever; my eyes and my heart will be there for all time. [17]And as for you, if you walk before me, as David your father walked, doing according to all that I have commanded you and keeping my statutes and my ordinances, [18]then I will establish your royal throne, as I covenanted with David your father, saying, 'There shall not fail you a man to rule Israel.'

[19]"But if you turn aside and forsake my statutes and my commandments which I have set before you, and go and serve other gods and worship them, [20]then I will pluck you up from the land which I have given you; and this house, which I have consecrated for my name, I will cast out of my sight, and will make it a proverb and a byword among all peoples. [21]And at this house, which is exalted, every one passing by will be astonished, and say, 'Why has the Lord done thus to this land and to this house?' [22]Then they will say, 'Because they forsook the Lord the God of their fathers who brought them out of the land of Egypt, and laid hold on other gods, and worshiped them and served them; therefore he has brought all this evil upon them.' "

Fire from heaven appears at the completion of the Temple as at the designation of the Temple site during David's reign (1 Chron 21:26). Great liturgical actions which go on for a fortnight follow this sign of the acceptance of the Temple, until Solomon sends the people away, "joyful and glad of heart for the goodness that the Lord had shown to David and to Solomon and to Israel his people" (vv.8-10).

The remainder of the chapter outlines God's response to Solomon's petitions; it is a response which stresses the covenant character of Israel's relationship with its God. His promises to answer his people's petitions are never mechanical; they are dependent on the people's own response, a response which is only manifested in their response to their fellow human beings as the ten commandments had long ago spelt out (cf. Deut 5). The kind of bargaining attitude which says: "I will say my prayers and do my bit of worship, if only you do such and such for me" was always condemned in Israel (cf. Amos 5:21-24; Jer 7) and the Chronicler, for all his emphasis on prayer and worship, does not negate this earlier attitude. The destruction of the First Temple had been a salutary reminder to the people of his time of the need to live thè covenant relationship to the full and not merely to pay lip service to it. But for those who repent of their evil ways, forgiveness is always assured. The emphasis on repentance will be very evident in the following sections of 2 Chronicles.

The completion of the Temple is linked to the completion of another great enterprise of Solomon's: the building of his own palace. 1 Kings mentions that this took thirteen years to build while the Temple only took seven (1 Kings 7:1-12). The description of the palace building is outlined in the same way in Kings as is the building of the Temple, whereas in Chronicles it is dismissed almost as an afterthought (v.11). Most of the remaining acts of Solomon's life are almost as summarily treated.

Various Acts of Solomon
8:1-18.

8 At the end of twenty years, in which Solomon had built the house of the Lord and his own house, ²Solomon rebuilt the cities which Huram had given to him, and settled the people of Israel in them.

³And Solomon went to Hamathzobah, and took it. ⁴He built Tadmor in the wilderness and all the store-cities which he built in Hamath. ⁵He also built Upper Bethhoron and Lower Bethhoron, fortified cities with walls, gates, and bars, ⁶and Baalath, and all the store-cities that Solomon had, and all the cities for his chariots, and the

cities for his horsemen, and whatever Solomon desired to build in Jerusalem, in Lebanon, and in all the land of his dominion. . . .

[11]Solomon brought Pharaoh's daughter up from the city of David to the house which he had built for her, for he said, "My wife shall not live in the house of David king of Israel, for the places to which the ark of the Lord has come are holy."

[12]Then Solomon offered up burnt offerings to the Lord upon the altar of the Lord which he had built before the vestibule, [13]as the duty of each day required, offering according to the commandment of Moses for the sabbaths, the new moons, and the three annual feasts—the feast of unleavened bread, the feast of weeks, and the feast of tabernacles. [14]According to the ordinance of David his father, he appointed the divisions of the priests for their service, and the Levites for their offices of praise and ministry before the priests as the duty of each day required, and the gatekeepers in their divisions for the several gates; for so David the man of God had commanded. [15]And they did not turn aside from what the king had commanded the priests and Levites concerning any matter and concerning the treasuries.

A summary of the remainder of Solomon's career is given in chapters eight and nine. The editorial work of the Chronicler is obvious. The transferal of the division of the country into administrative districts from Solomon's reign (1 Kings 4) to that of David can be noted (1 Chron 27). Also remarkable is the fact that Solomon is said to have received cities from Huram of Tyre while Kings implies that he actually had to cede these cities. It is historically accurate that the kingdom of Israel actually shrank during the reign of Solomon but this was not in accord with the traditional image of Solomon as head of a great Empire. It is this latter image which is uppermost in Chronicles (cf. 9:26).

There is also an interesting development in the treatment of Pharaoh's daughter. In Kings, it is as a mark of honour that she is removed from the city of David to a new palace especially built for her, while in Chronicles it is a question of ritual impurity which prompts her removal. The Chronicler, however, omits the section of Kings dealing with the sins of Solomon from his contact with foreign wives. This is in line with his policy of omitting, as for David, the seamier side of Solomon's career.

In contrast to the military exploits of David, Solomon's one and only war stands out (v.3). It is not actually mentioned in Kings. Solomon was better as a builder than as a warrior and a record of the cities he either built or rebuilt is staggering. He also dabbled in ship-building (vv.17-18), though the reminiscences of this activity were rather vague as Israel was not able to hold on to ports like Eziongeber on the gulf of Aqabah. Even in this chapter of more secular activities his concern with the cult and its personnel does not escape mention (vv.12-16).

Solomon's Wealth and Wisdom
9:1-31.

9 Now when the queen of Sheba heard of the fame of Solomon she came to Jerusalem to test him with hard questions, having a very great retinue and camels bearing spices and very much gold and precious stones. When she came to Solomon, she told him all that was on her mind...

22Thus King Solomon excelled all the kings of the earth in riches and in wisdom. 23And all the kings of the earth sought the presence of Solomon to hear his wisdom, which God had put into his mind. 24Every one of them brought his present, articles of silver and of gold, garments, myrrh, spices, horses, and mules, so much year by year. 25And Solomon had four thousand stalls for horses and chariots, and twelve thousand horsemen, whom he stationed in the chariot cities and with the king in Jerusalem. 26And he ruled over all the kings from the Euphrates to the land of the Philistines, and to the border of Egypt. 27And the king made silver as common in Jerusalem as stone, and cedar as plentiful as the sycamore of the Shephelah. [28]And horses were imported for Solomon from Egypt and from all lands.

[29]Now the rest of the acts of Solomon, from first to last, are they not written in the history of Nathan the prophet, and in the prophecy of Ahijah the Shilonite, and in the visions of Iddo the seer concerning Jeroboam the son of Nebat? [30]Solomon reigned in Jerusalem over all Israel forty years. [31]And Solomon slept with his fathers, and was buried in the city of David his father; and Rehoboam his son reigned in his stead.

The Queen of Sheba's visit to Solomon was probably in the nature of a trade mission necessitated by the advent of a new arrival on the international scene who was posing a threat to a long-standing monopoly. Lavish compliments and presents were exchanged, the famed wisdom was admired and she returned home duly mollified. It has been suggested that this visit and others like it (e.g. vv.23-24) have the character of the prophetic indrawing of all the nations of Jerusalem (cf. Is 60). This is the magnet rather than the ghetto image of Jerusalem which was spoken about in the Introduction. It is portrayed as fully operative during the reign of the ideal king, Solomon.

The story of Solomon ends with the usual indication of other possible sources for knowledge about his deeds. At least two of these, that of Nathan and Ahijah, probably refer to material found in Kings. The "prophecy of Ahijah the Shilonite. . . concerning Jeroboam the son of Nebat" predicted that some of the kingdom would be taken from Solomon's successors and given to Jeroboam because of Solomon's apostasy at the end of his life (1 Kings 11). This material was omitted by the Chronicler because it cast Solomon in an unfavourable light but that he was aware of it is indicated by his mention of the source here. The "visions of Iddo" were presumably in similar vein.

IV. GOOD AND BAD KINGS IN JUDAH 2 Chron 10:1—36:23.

THE DIVISION OF DAVID'S KINGDOM
10:1—11:4

10 Rehoboam went to Shechem, for all Israel had come to Shechem to make him king. [2]And when Jeroboam the son of Nebat heard of it (for he was in Egypt, whither he had fled from King Solomon), then Jeroboam returned from Egypt. [3]And they sent and called him; and Jeroboam and all Israel came and said to Rehoboam, [4]"Your father made our yoke heavy. Now therefore lighten the hard service of your father and his heavy yoke upon us, and we will serve you." [5]He said to them, "Come to me again in three days." So the people went away.

[6]Then King Rehoboam took counsel with the old men, who had stood before Solomon his father while he was yet alive, saying, "How do you advise me to answer this people?" [7]And they said to him, "If you will be kind to this people and please them, and speak good words to them, then they will be your servants for ever." [8]But he forsook the counsel which the old men gave him, and took counsel with the young men who had grown up with him and stood before him. [9]And he said to them, "What do you advise that we answer this people who have said to me, 'Lighten the yoke that your father put upon us'?" [10]And the young men who had grown up with him said to him,

"Thus shall you speak to the people who said to you, 'Your father made our yoke heavy, but do you lighten it for us'; thus shall you say to them, 'My little finger is thicker than my father's loins. 11And now, whereas my father laid upon you a heavy yoke, I will add to your yoke. My father chastised you with whips, but I will chastise you with scorpions.' "

12So Jeroboam and all the people came to Rehoboam the third day, as the king said, "Come to me again the third day." 13And the king answered them harshly, and forsaking the counsel of the old men....

16And when all Israel saw that the king did not hearken to them, the people answered the king,

"What portion have we in David?

We have no inheritance in the son of Jesse.

Each of you to your tents, O Israel!

Look now to your own house, David."

So all Israel departed to their tents. 17But Rehoboam reigned over the people of Israel who dwelt in the cities of Judah. 18Then King Rehoboam sent Hadoram, who was taskmaster over the forced labor, and the people of Israel stoned him to death with stones. And King Rehoboam made haste to mount his chariot, to flee to Jerusalem. 19So Israel has been in rebellion against the house of David to this day.

11 When Rehoboam came to Jerusalem, he assembled the house of Judah, and Benjamin, a hundred and eighty thousand chosen warriors, to fight against Israel, to restore the kingdom to Rehoboam. 2But the word of the Lord came to Shemaiah the man of God: 3"Say to Rehoboam the son of Solomon king of Judah, and to all Israel in Judah and Benjamin, 4"Thus says the Lord, You shall not go up or fight against your brethren. Return every man to his home, for this thing is from me.'" So they hearkened to the word of the Lord, and returned and did not go against Jeroboam.

The personal linking of all twelve tribes under David falls

apart after the death of Solomon. Rehoboam, his son, presumably crowned king of Judah, and Benjamin to the south needed to be ratified by the ten northern tribes but failed to win acceptance because of his high-handed policy. Underlying the episode is the strong dissatisfaction caused in Solomon's time by heavy taxation to finance his extensive building operations. The traditions of the desert and the Exodus were stronger in the North so when a new leader emerged "out of Egypt" (1 Kings 11:40) they preferred him to a son of the house of David.

The Chronicler is prepared to acknowledge the legitimacy of the North's grievance against Rehoboam. Judgment on the matter comes to the king through Shemaiah, "the man of God" (11:2-4). In the section of Chronicles just beginning, intervention of prophets as carriers of the word of God is very frequent. They are the living conscience of the people. Even though the division has occurred between the tribes the Northerners are still "your brothers" (v.4). The most striking difference between the books of Kings and Chronicles in this section of the history of Israel is the omission of almost every reference to the Northern Kingdom in Chronicles. Because of this it was commonplace among scholars in the past to speak of the Chronicler's love of Judah (as the South came to be called) and of his hatred for Israel (the North), but recent studies on the use of the term, *Israel,* in Chronicles have shown that the whole people are still, even after the split, considered as one. Phrases like "Israel," "all Israel," "sons of Israel" can be applied to the North or to the South or even to both together, though the phrase, "house of Israel" is reserved to the North. The Chronicler's contention will be with the Northern kings as such rather than with its people who are still to him, "children of God."

REHOBOAM'S REIGN
11:5—12:16

> ⁵Rehoboam dwelt in Jerusalem, and he built cities for defense in Judah....
> ¹³And the priests and the Levites that were in all Israel

resorted to him from all places where they lived, [14]For the Levites left their common lands and their holdings and came to Judah and Jerusalem, because Jeroboam and his sons cast them out from serving as priests of the Lord, [15]and he appointed his own priests for the high places, and for the satyrs, and for the calves which he had made. [16]And those who had set their hearts to seek the Lord God of Israel came after them from all the tribes of Israel to Jerusalem to sacrifice to the Lord, the God of their fathers....

12 When the rule of Rehoboam was established and was strong, he forsook the law of the Lord, and all Israel with him. [2]In the fifth year of King Rehoboam, because they had been unfaithful to the Lord, Shishak king of Egypt came up against Jerusalem [3]with twelve hundred chariots and sixty thousand horsemen. And the people were without number who came with him from Egypt— Libyans, Sukkiim, and Ethiopians. [4]And he took the fortified cities of Judah and came as far as Jerusalem. [5]Then Shemaiah the prophet came to Rehoboam and to the princes of Judah, who had gathered at Jerusalem because of Shishak, and said to them, "Thus says the Lord, 'You abandoned me, so I have abandoned you to the hand of Shishak' " [6]Then the princes of Israel and the king humbled themselves and said, "The Lord is righteous." [7]When the Lord saw that they humbled themselves, the word of the Lord came to Shemaiah: "They have humbled themselves; I will not destroy them, but I will grant them some deliverance, and my wrath shall not be poured out upon Jerusalem by the hand of Shishak. [8]Nevertheless they shall be servants to him, that they may know my service and the service of the kingdoms of the countries."...

[15]Now the acts of Rehoboam, from first to last, are they not written in the chronicles of Shemaiah the prophet and of Iddo the seer? There were continual wars between Rehoboam and Jeroboam. [16]And Rehoboam slept with his fathers, and was buried in the city of David; and Abijah his son reigned in his stead.

These chapters contain much valuable supplementary material to Kings on the state of the country at the end of the tenth century B.C. The Chronicler elaborates on the campaign of the Egyptian Pharaoh, Shishak, and on the line of fortifications built by Rehoboam as a result. These accounts have been verified by the archaeological discovery of an inscription of Shishak which lists all the cities in Judah which he conquered. Jerusalem is not mentioned among them and this is in accord with the statement in 12:4 which merely says that he "came as far as Jerusalem" and with the obvious giving of tribute in verse nine. Excavations on many of the sites mentioned in 11:5-10 also confirm the presence of fortifications at this particular time. Sections like this bear witness to the exceptional accuracy of much of the Chronicler's additional material.

But at the same time it would be true to say that the Chronicler was not the least bit interested in archaeology. His main purpose in this section is to assess the conduct of both Jeroboam and Rehoboam in the light of the people's covenant relationship to God. Both are found wanting — Jeroboam, because of his leading the people astray into alien worship at illegitimate shrines; Rehoboam, because he "forsook the law of God." But the latter at least repents on being told of God's anger against him by the prophet, Shemaiah (12:1-8). This section is a clear example of the Chronicler's doctrine of retribution: sin evokes immediate punishment, a punishment which is called off, or at least modified, by repentance. This pattern will be evident in much of the subsequent history of the kings of Judah.

THE SUCCESS OF GOOD KINGS
13:1—20:37

Abijah
13:1-22

13 In the eighteenth year of King Jeroboam Abijah began to reign over Judah. ²He reigned for three years in

Jerusalem. His mother's name was Micaiah the daughter of Uriel of Gibeah.

Now there was war between Abijah and Jeroboam. ³Abijah went out to battle having an army of valiant men of war, four hundred thousand picked men; and Jeroboam drew up his line of battle against him with eight hundred thousand picked mighty warriors. ⁴Then Abijah stood up on Mount Zemaraim which is in the hill country of Ephraim, and said, "Hear me, O Jeroboam and all Israel! ⁵Ought you not to know that the Lord God of Israel gave the kingship over Israel for ever to David and his sons by a covenant of salt? ⁶Yet Jeroboam the son of Nebat, a servant of Solomon the son of David, rose up and rebelled against his lord; ⁷and certain worthless scoundrels gathered about him and defied Rehoboam the son of Solomon, when Rehoboam was young and irresolute and could not withstand them.

⁸"And now you think to withstand the kingdom of the Lord in the hand of the sons of David, because you are a great multitude and have with you the golden calves which Jeroboam made you for gods. ⁹Have you not driven out the priests of the Lord, the sons of Aaron, and the Levites, and made priests for yourselves like the peoples of other lands? Whoever comes to consecrate himself with a young bull or seven rams becomes a priest of what are no gods. ¹⁰But as for us, the Lord is our God, and we have not forsaken him. We have priests ministering to the Lord who are sons of Aaron, and Levites for their service. ¹¹They offer to the Lord every morning and every evening burnt offerings and incense of sweet spices, set out the showbread on the table of pure gold, and care for the golden lampstand that its lamps may burn every evening; for we keep the charge of the Lord our God, but you have forsaken him. ¹²Behold, God is with us at our head, and his priests with their battle trumpets to sound the call to battle against you. O sons of Israel, do not fight against the Lord, the God of your fathers; for you cannot succeed."

¹³Jeroboam had sent an ambush around to come on them from behind; thus his troops were in front of Judah, and the ambush was behind them. ¹⁴And when Judah looked, behold, the battle was before and behind them; and they cried to the Lord, and the priests blew the trumpets. ¹⁵Then the men of Judah raised the battle shout. And when the men of Judah shouted, God defeated Jeroboam and all Israel before Abijah and Judah.

The favourable judgment of the Chronicler on Abijah is very different from that of Kings. He is in fact the mouthpiece for the best exposition of the Chronicler's theology in the whole work whereas in Kings he is treated as a nonentity. The theological treatise here takes the form of a levitical sermon inserted into the narrative of Abijah's offensive against the North (see Intro. p. 2, 6). It has been variously described as Abijah's "sermon on the mount" or the "magna carta of the Jewish monopoly of salvation." This latter is hardly a fair judgment on the speech. Its point lies elsewhere. In chapter eleven it was clear that the Chronicler appreciated the fact that the Northerners would find it difficult to follow Rehoboam. What he is saying now seems to be that after Rehoboam's death there was no excuse for staying away from Jerusalem because, after all, the Davidic king was the viceroy of God (the covenant of salt in verse five seems to signify the perpetuity of this covenant, cf. Num 18:19). Instead of returning, however, the people have followed the apostate king, Jeroboam, into rebellion — into a cult which is false and offered by a priesthood which has no claim to authenticity, all the legitimate priests and Levites having made their way to Jerusalem.

It is obvious that here, as always, the Chronicler has one eye on the people of his own time and is using this historical episode to speak out against the syncretistic worship then in vogue. The fact that Abijah had right on his side is proved, for the Chronicler, by his success in battle. The battle is described in terms reminiscent of the Books of Joshua and Judges: Abijah prevails even though he has only half the numbers of his opponents and even though he is hemmed in on every side. The battle is a practical illustration of the constant call to the people to put their trust in God rather than in weapons and allies (cf. Is 30:15-18).

Asa
14:1—16:14.

14 So Abijah slept with his fathers, and they buried him in the city of David; and Asa his son reigned in his stead. In his days the land had rest for ten years. ²And Asa did what was good and right in the eyes of the Lord. . . .
15 ¹⁶Even Maacah, his mother, King Asa removed from being queen mother because she had made an abominable image for Asherah. Asa cut down her image, crushed it, and burned it at the brook Kidron. ¹⁷But the high places were not taken out of Israel. Nevertheless the heart of Asa was blameless all his days. ¹⁸And he brought into the house of God the votive gifts of his father and his own votive gifts, silver, and gold, and vessels. ¹⁹And there was no more war until the thirty-fifth year of the reign of Asa.
16 In the thirty-sixth year of the reign of Asa, Baasha king of Israel went up against Judah, and built Ramah, that he might permit no one to go out or come in to Asa king of Judah. ²Then Asa took silver and gold from the treasures of the house of the Lord and the king's house, and sent them to Benhadad king of Syria, who dwelt in Damascus, saying, ³"Let there be a league between me and you, as between my father and your father; behold, I am sending to you silver and gold; go, break your league with Baasha king of Israel, that he may withdraw from me.". . .

⁷At that time Hanani the seer came to Asa king of Judah, and said to him, "Because you relied on the king of Syria, and did not rely on the Lord your God, the army of the king of Syria has escaped you. ⁸Were not the Ethiopians and the Libyans a huge army with exceedingly

many chariots and horsemen? Yet because you relied on
the Lord, he gave them into your hand. [9]For the eyes of
the Lord run to and fro throughout the whole earth, to
show his might in behalf of those whose heart is blameless toward him. You have done foolishly in this; for from
now on you will have wars." [10]Then Asa was angry with
the seer, and put him in the stocks, in prison, for he was in
a rage with him because of this. And Asa inflicted cruel-
ties upon some of the people at the same time.

[11]The acts of Asa, from first to last, are written in the
Book of the Kings of Judah and Israel. [12]In the thirty-
ninth year of his reign Asa was diseased in his feet, and his
disease became severe; yet even in his disease he did not
seek the Lord, but sought help from physicians.

Asa's career also illustrates the Chronicler's point that if a
king depends totally upon God he will be successful against
his enemies (14:9-13); if not, he will be punished (16:7-12). At
the beginning of his reign Asa followed in the footsteps of
Abijah; he was a religious reformer who tried to eliminate
the worship of idols from the land. Reading between the
lines of the Books of Chronicles, and indeed of most other
books of the Bible, one is forced to wonder how the worship
of Yahweh survived at all in Israel. Time and time again,
king, people and even priests seemed quite content with a
syncretistic version of their religion in which various other
gods were worshipped alongside Yahweh or, if he was worshipped at all, it was often under the characteristics of these
other gods.

One of the chief offenders at this time was the Queen
Mother (15:16). The Queen Mother was often a very important person in the court of the king. She could be chief
counselor and often acted as regent, for example if the king
were not of age. This may have been the case at the beginning of Asa's reign. There is some confusion as to whether
Maacah was the mother or grandmother of Asa (cf.13:2).
Either way she was probably a formidable lady and going
against the fashions she had set in religious matters must

have taken no small degree of courage on the part of the young king (15:8).

The result of his reform was a great renewal of the covenant between God and the people. This recalls the account in Joshua 24 of the great covenant renewal ceremony at Shechem and is followed by a period of peace as was also said to be the case after Shechem. Asa uses this period of peace to build fortifications. This ensured prosperity, a prosperity envied by the neighbouring king of Israel, Baasha, who in an endeavour to stop those of his own people who were increasingly attracted to Jerusalem (perhaps for business as much as for worship) sets up a border post at Ramah. Artificial borders have always caused trouble.

This move robs Asa of his serenity. He promptly tries to undermine Baasha by cutting in on his ally to the north, Benhadad of Syria, bribing him to break his word to Baasha. This, unfortunately for Asa, provokes a strong prophetic rebuke at home which warns him that his lack of trust in God has put an end to his peace.

It is interesting to note that prophetic interventions in this section of Chronicles are not in the form of new prophecies but rather preachings on prophetic and other texts of the Bible which were already well established. Here Ps 33:13 immediately comes to mind: "The Lord looks down from heaven, he sees all the sons of men," as well as many passages in Isaiah (cf. 30:1-7; 15-17; 31:1-3). Asa does not take too kindly to the prophet's words and makes him suffer for his pains. There may be a direct link between this ill-treatment and the subsequent fact that Asa is afflicted with a disease of the feet. He is castigated by the Chronicler for depending on physicians in his illness rather than on God. This cannot be used as a text condemning all recourse to medicine; very often in ancient times, medicine and magic were mixed. It is rather a call to see God as the one who punishes but who also heals (Hos 6:1).

Jehoshaphat
17:1—20:37.

17 Jehoshaphat his son reigned in his stead, and strengthened himself against Israel. [2]He placed forces in all the fortified cities of Judah, and set garrisons in the land of Judah, and in the cities of Ephraim which Asa his father had taken. [3]The Lord was with Jehoshaphat, because he walked in the earlier ways of his father; he did not seek the Baals, [4]but sought the God of his father and walked in his commandments, and not according to the ways of Israel. . . .

[10]And the fear of the Lord fell upon all the kingdoms of the lands that were round about Judah, and they made no war against Jehoshaphat. [11]Some of the Philistines brought Jehoshaphat presents, and silver for tribute; and the Arabs also brought him seven thousand seven hundred rams and seven thousand seven hundred he-goats. . . .

18 Now Jehoshaphat had great riches and honor; and he made a marriage alliance with Ahab. [2]After some years he went down to Ahab in Samaria. And Ahab killed an abundance of sheep and oxen for him and for the people who were with him, and induced him to go up against Ramoth-gilead. [3]Ahab king of Israel said to Jehoshaphat king of Judah, "Will you go with me to Ramoth-gilead?" He answered him, "I am as you are, my people as your people. We will be with you in the war.". . .

[28]So the king of Israel and Jehoshaphat the king of Judah went up to Ramoth-gilead. [29]And the king of Israel said to Jehoshaphat, "I will disguise myself and go into battle but you wear your robes." And the king of Israel disguised himself; and they went into battle. [30]Now the king of Syria had commanded the captains of his chariots, "Fight with neither small nor great, but only with the king of Israel." [31]And when the captains of the chariots saw Jehoshaphat, they said, "It is the king of Israel." So they turned to fight against him; and Jehoshaphat cried out, and the Lord helped him. God drew them away from him, [32]for when the captains of the chariots saw that it

was not the king of Israel, they turned back from pursuing him. ³³But a certain man drew his bow at a venture, and struck the king of Israel between the scale armor and the breastplate; therefore he said to the driver of his chariot, "Turn about, and carry me out of the battle, for I am wounded." ³⁴And the battle grew hot that day, and the king of Israel propped himself up in his chariot facing the Syrians until evening; then at sunset he died.

19 Jehoshaphat the king of Judah returned in safety to his house in Jerusalem. ²But Jehu the son of Hanani the seer went out to meet him, and said to King Jehoshaphat, "Should you help the wicked and love those who hate the Lord? Because of this, wrath has gone out against you from the Lord. ³Nevertheless some good is found in you, for you destroyed the Asherahs out of the land, and have set your heart to seek God."

Jehoshaphat was one of the Chronicler's favourite kings. His name means "Yahweh judges" and he is portrayed as zealous for the justice of God, seeking his ways and making known his commandments. Because of this, and in keeping with the theory of the Chronicler, he is obviously successful and honoured in the eyes of the nations. His religious attitudes, however, are not purely personal: like his father before him, and every other faithful Israelite king, he cares for his people by ensuring their safety and prosperity (17:2; 12-13).

His one blind spot was his alliance with the northern king, Ahab. This led him into a rather difficult situation from which he was released only because of his recognition of a true prophet of God, one who withstood the false prophets whom Ahab cultivated. In characteristic fashion, the Chronicler does not give much detail about northern affairs and only tells this story because of the involvement of a southern king. But his abhorrence of Ahab and his house comes through at several junctures (cf. 21:6; 22:2-3). Ahab, spurred on by his non-Israelite wife, Jezebel (cf. 1 Kings 16:31) encouraged the worship of Baal, the semitic god who posed

the strongest threat to the worship of Israel's God, Yahweh.
Here lies the Chronicler's basic antipathy to the North: not
to the people as a whole who still remain brothers of Judah
and children of God, but to the northern kings who lead the
people into apostasy.

To drive home the lesson, another prophet meets Jehoshaphat after his providential escape (19:1-3). It is a message
which is reminiscent of the Psalmist's contention that those
who walk in the ways of the Lord should not mix with
evildoers (cf. Ps 1). The warning comes from the milieu of
post-exilic times where belief in God was in danger of being
swamped by foreign ideas which were flowing freely
through the land at that time in the wake of passing soldiers,
statesmen and traders of the Persian Empire. The Chronicler, then, is again using a historical event to speak to the
people of his own time.

The reaction of keeping away from the "wicked" in the
interests of survival was a natural one and it is possible that
Judaism would have been obliterated totally in the cosmo-
politan world of the time if at least some within the fold had
not reacted as the Chronicler and the Psalmist. An intensifi-
cation of this separatist attitude will be apparent in Ezra and
Nehemiah. The other side of the coin can be seen in parts of
the Wisdom literature of the Bible where a cautious wel-
come is given to the currents of new thinking. This assimila-
tionist tendency was also part of the post-exilic world and
often in conflict with the more separatist attitudes of Chronicles, Ezra and Nehemiah.

Jehoshaphat the Reformer
17:7-9; 19:4-11.

> **17** ⁷In the third year of his reign he sent his princes,
> Benhail, Obadiah, Zechariah, Nethanel, and Micaiah,
> to teach in the cities of Judah; ⁸and with them the Levites,
> Shemaiah, Nethaniah, Zebadiah, Asahel, Shemiramoth,
> Jehonathan, Adonijah, Tobijah, and Tobadonijah; and
> with these Levites, the priests Elishama and Jehoram.
> ⁹And they taught in Judah, having the book of the law

of the Lord with them; they went about through all the cities of Judah and taught among the people. . . .

19 ⁴Jehoshaphat dwelt at Jerusalem; and he went out again among the people, from Beer-sheba to the hill country of Ephraim, and brought them back to the Lord, the God of their fathers. ⁵He appointed judges in the land in all the fortified cities of Judah, city by city, ⁶and said to the judges, "Consider what you do, for you judge not for man but for the Lord; he is with you in giving judgment. ⁷Now then, let the fear of the Lord be upon you; take heed what you do, for there is no perversion of justice with the Lord our God, or partiality, or taking bribes."

⁸Moreover in Jerusalem Jehoshaphat appointed certain Levites and priests and heads of families of Israel, to give judgment for the Lord and to decide disputed cases. They had their seat at Jerusalem. ⁹And he charged them: "Thus you shall do in the fear of the Lord, in faithfulness, and with your whole heart: ¹⁰whenever a case comes to you from your brethren who live in their cities, concerning bloodshed, law or commandment, statutes or ordinances, then you shall instruct them, that they may not incur guilt before the Lord and wrath may not come upon you and your brethren. Thus you shall do, and you will not incur guilt. ¹¹And behold, Amariah the chief priest is over you in all matters of the Lord; and Zebadiah the son of Ishmael, the governor of the house of Judah, in all the king's matters; and the Levites will serve you as officers. Deal courageously, and may the Lord be with the upright!"

Jehoshaphat was one of the great reformers of Israel, along with Hezekiah and Josiah. Getting rid of false centres of worship was necessary in every age of Israel's history and the Chronicler is probably accurate in recording several attempts at reform as against Kings where reform is reserved to the time of Josiah alone (cf. 2 Kings 22; 2 Chron 34). The thrust of Jehoshaphat's reform was three-pronged:

a) For the first time notice is given that the high places and the Asherim are completely removed (17:6). These Asherim were the cult symbols of a female fertility goddess, Asherah, and they exerted a strong influence on the people as was evidenced earlier in their being cultivated by a Queen Mother (cf. 15:16).

b) Princes and Levites are sent all over the country to teach "the book of the law of the Lord" (17:7-9). In speaking of the "book of the law of the Lord," the Chronicler is probably thinking of the law of his own day as taught and explained by the Levites (cf. Neh 8). The mention of princes suggests a strong military escort which probably reflects the situation in earlier Israel where religious reform would have been carried through by military strength, while the mention of levitical teaching is more in keeping with the Chronicler's own time.

c) A reform of the judiciary at local centres and in Jerusalem itself follows. There is a strong condemnation of partiality in judgment and of the taking of bribes (cf. Ex 23:1-3; 6-8; Deut 16:18-20). In Jerusalem, as well as the local court, there was to be a court of appeal over which the chief priest would preside in religious matters and an appointee of the king in civil affairs. The division between religious and secular affairs again reflects the later period as does the handing over of the powers of chief justice by the king (cf. 1 Chron 18:14).

Victory From the Lord
20:1-37.

> **20** After this the Moabites and Ammonites, and with them some of the Meunites, came against Jehoshaphat for battle. . . .
>
> ⁵And Jehoshaphat stood in the assembly of Judah and Jerusalem, in the house of the Lord, before the new court, ⁶and said, "O Lord, God of our fathers, art thou not God in heaven? Dost thou not rule over all the kingdoms of the nations? In thy hand are power and might, so that none is

able to withstand thee. [7]Didst thou not, O our God, drive out the inhabitants of this land before thy people Israel, and give it for ever to the descendants of Abraham thy friend? [8]And they have dwelt in it, and have built thee in it a sanctuary for thy name, saying, [9]"If evil comes upon us, the sword, judgment, or pestilence, or famine, we will stand before this house, and before thee, for thy name is in this house, and cry to thee in our affliction, and thou wilt hear and save.' [10]And now behold, the men of Ammon and Moab and Mount Seir, whom thou wouldest not let Israel invade when they came from the land of Egypt, and whom they avoided and did not destroy — [11]behold, they reward us by coming to drive us out of thy possession, which thou hast given us to inherit. [12]O our God, wilt thou not execute judgment upon them? For we are powerless against this great multitude that is coming against us. We do not know what to do, but our eyes are upon thee.". . .

[20]And they rose early in the morning and went out into the wilderness of Tekoa; and as they went out, Jehoshaphat stood and said, "Hear me, Judah and inhabitants of Jerusalem! Believe in the Lord your God, and you will be established; believe his prophets, and you will succeed." [21]And when he had taken counsel with the people, he appointed those who were to sing to the Lord and praise him in holy array, as they went before the army, and say,
  "Give thanks to the Lord,
     for his steadfast love endures for ever."
[22]And when they began to sing and praise, the Lord set an ambush against the men of Ammon, Moab, and Mount Seir, who had come against Judah, so that they were routed. [23]For the men of Ammon and Moab rose against the inhabitants of Mount Seir, destroying them utterly, and when they had made an end of the inhabitants of Seir, they all helped to destroy one another. . . .

[34]Now the rest of the acts of Jehoshaphat, from first to last, are written in the chronicles of Jehu the son of Hanani, which are recorded in the Book of the Kings of Israel.

³⁵After this Jehoshaphat king of Judah joined with Ahaziah king of Israel, who did wickedly. ³⁶He joined him in building ships to go to Tarshish, and they built the ships in Eziongeber. ³⁷Then Eliezer the son of Dodavahu of Mareshah prophesied against Jehoshaphat, saying, "Because you have joined with Ahaziah, the Lord will destroy what you have made." And the ships were wrecked and were not able to go to Tarshish.

This chapter is a good example of the Chronicler's method of dealing with history. The ancient world did not know the meaning of objective history (if there is such a thing) and the recounting of history always had another purpose in mind. The Chronicler's purpose here is to use historical narrative to get across to the people of his own time the value of trusting in God. There is no doubt that a historical battle did take place in Jehoshaphat's lifetime (cf. 1 Kings 22:45), but the passage here is more a parable in action than an actual historical account of that battle. The Chronicler's sole purpose is to show that direct divine intervention is to be expected in answer to prayer and praise (20:22). The prayer of Jehoshaphat before the battle takes up the petitions of Solomon at the dedication of the Temple (6:18-42). God will listen to his people in their necessity.

In his address to the people, Jehoshaphat himself takes on the role of a prophet. As in the prophetic interventions noted in earlier chapters, he preaches on known texts from the great prophets. This time it is the famous text from Isaiah: "If you do not stand by me you will not stand at all" (Is 7:9; Jerusalem Bible version). He uses it to exhort the people to a firm faith and confidence in God. This type of preaching was typical of the levitical sermon (see Intro. p. 6); here its use is extended to the king himself.

The final word on Jehoshaphat is slightly judgmental because he again gets himself entangled with a northern king (20:35-37). This time it was in a business enterprise. It was doomed to failure from the start, because any dealings with the heretical kingship of the North involved one in its condemnation (cf. 2 Chron 13:4-12).

THE FAILURE OF BAD KINGS (AND A QUEEN) 21:1—23:21

Jehoram
21:1—21:20

21 Jehoshaphat slept with his fathers, and was buried with his fathers in the city of David; and Jehoram his son reigned in his stead. ²He had brothers, the sons of Jehoshaphat: Azariah, Jehiel, Zechariah, Azariah, Michael, and Shephatiah; all these were the sons of Jehoshaphat king of Judah. ³Their father gave them great gifts, of silver, gold, and valuable possessions, together with fortified cities in Judah; but he gave the kingdom to Jehoram, because he was the first-born. ⁴When Jehoram had ascended the throne of his father and was established, he slew all his brothers with the sword, and also some of the princes of Israel. ⁵Jehoram was thirty-two years old when he became king, and he reigned eight years in Jerusalem. ⁶And he walked in the way of the kings of Israel, as the house of Ahab had done; for the daughter of Ahab was his wife. And he did what was evil in the sight of the Lord. ⁷Yet the Lord would not destroy the house of David, because of the covenant which he had made with David, and since he had promised to give a lamp to him and to his sons for ever. . . .

¹²And a letter came to him from Elijah the prophet, saying, "Thus says the Lord, the God of David your father, 'Because you have not walked in the ways of Jehoshaphat your father, or in the ways of Asa king of Judah, ¹³but have walked in the way of the kings of Israel, and have led Judah and the inhabitants of Jerusalem into unfaithfulness, as the house of Ahab led Israel into unfaithfulness, and also you have killed your brothers, of your father's house, who were better than yourself;

¹⁴behold, the Lord will bring a great plague on your people, your children, your wives, and all your possessions, ¹⁵and you yourself will have a severe sickness with a disease of your bowels, until your bowels come out because of the disease, day by day.'"

The reign of the next king, Jehoram, is in complete contrast to that of Jehoshaphat. The result of not walking in the ways of the Lord is clearly evident in the account of this reign: strife, defeat at the hands of neighbouring kingdoms, plague among the people at home and finally a debilitating personal disease which brings the king to an early grave. In this, and in subsequent chapters, the Chronicler's insistence that wickedness brings its own immediate punishment is clearly spelt out. Saul, for him, had been the first example of such retribution (1 Chron 10) and Rehoboam had exemplified it to a certain extent (2 Chron 10) but this section of Chronicles will make his point abundantly clear. In the case of Jehoram it is evident that his downfall was to be expected given his close connections with the apostate house of Ahab to the North.

Jehoram's only redeeming feature was that he at least kept the line of David on the throne. To ensure that he was the one who would do this he had all his brothers killed on his accession to the throne. The later murder of his own sons could be seen as a judgment on his murderous activities. His actions provoked strong criticism from an unexpected quarter in the form of a letter from Elijah, the great prophet of the Northern kingdom, the "troubler of Israel," as Ahab called him (1 Kings 18:17). This is the only reference to Elijah in Chronicles in spite of the fact that Kings devoted about six chapters to his activities. There is no reference to the letter in any of these chapters. Since Elijah had disappeared from the scene before the reign of Jehoram's contemporary in the North (cf. 2 Kings 2, 3), it is felt that what is involved here is the Chronicler's wish to identify with Elijah's stand for Yahweh. The condemnation of Jehoram is in accord with the other prophetic interventions against the kings of Judah.

Ahaziah
22:1-9.

22   And the inhabitants of Jerusalem made Ahaziah his youngest son king in his stead; for the band of men that came with the Arabs to the camp had slain all the older sons. So Ahaziah the son of Jehoram king of Judah reigned. ²Ahaziah was forty-two years old when he began to reign, and he reigned one year in Jerusalem. His mother's name was Athaliah, the granddaughter of Omri. ³He also walked in the ways of the house of Ahab, for his mother was his counselor in doing wickedly. ⁴He did what was evil in the sight of the Lord, as the house of Ahab had done; for after the death of his father they were his counselors, to his undoing. ⁵He even followed their counsel, and went with Jehoram the son of Ahab king of Israel to make war against Hazael king of Syria at Ramoth-gilead. And the Syrians wounded Joram, ⁶and he returned to be healed in Jezreel of the wounds which he had received at Ramah, when he fought against Hazael king of Syria. And Ahaziah the son of Jehoram king of Judah went down to see Joram the son of Ahab in Jezreel, because he was sick.

⁷But is was ordained by God that the downfall of Ahaziah should come about through his going to visit Joram. For when he came there he went out with Jehoram to meet Jehu the son of Nimshi, whom the Lord had anointed to destroy the house of Ahab. ⁸And when Jehu was executing judgment upon the house of Ahab, he met the princes of Judah and the sons of Ahaziah's brothers, who attended Ahaziah, and he killed them. ⁹He searched for Ahaziah, and he was captured while hiding in Samaria, and he was brought to Jehu and put to death. They buried him, for they said, "He is the grandson of Jehoshaphat, who sought the Lord with all his heart." And the house of Ahaziah had no one able to rule the kingdom.

There is a problem about the age of the next king of Israel, Ahaziah. The text has forty-two years here though the Greek translation has twenty, while the corresponding passage in Kings has twenty-two. Either of these latter figures would be more acceptable since if he was forty-two, he would have been two years older than his father who had just died (21:5). The rot which had set in under Jehoram continues under Ahaziah. The influence of the house of Ahab is still all persuasive in the person of Ahaziah's mother, Athaliah. She was Ahab's daughter or, as the text puts it, the granddaughter of Omri. It was Omri, the father of Ahab, who had founded the line of kings in the North which was so abhorrent to the Chronicler (cf. 1 Kings 16).

Ahaziah was totally under the influence of northern advisers and his involvement in the affairs of the North was greater than that of any other king of Judah. It was this involvement which brought about his death since he was so totally identified with the house of Ahab that he was swept along in its overthrow by one Jehu, the son of Nimshi (cf. 2 Kings 9, 10). At Ahaziah's end there is a touching pointer to the fact that the Chronicler believed in the faithfulness to God of many in the North in spite of the apostasy of their kings. He portrays the people as giving Ahaziah a decent burial for the sake of his grandfather, Jehoshaphat, who sought the Lord with "all his heart" (v.9).

Athaliah
22:10—23:21.

¹⁰Now when Athaliah the mother of Ahaziah saw that her son was dead, she arose and destroyed all the royal family of the house of Judah. ¹¹But Jehoshabeath, the daughter of the king, took Joash the son of Ahaziah, and stole him away from among the king's sons who were about to be slain, and she put him and his nurse in a bedchamber. Thus Jehoshabeath, the daughter of King Jehoram and wife of Jehoiada the priest, because she was a sister of Ahaziah, hid him from Athaliah, so that she did not slay him; ¹²and he remained with them six years, hid

in the house of God, while Athaliah reigned over the land. **23** But in the seventh year Jehoiada took courage, and entered into a compact with the commanders of hundreds...

⁸The Levites and all Judah did according to all that Jehoiada the priest commanded. They each brought his men, who were to go off duty on the sabbath, with those who were to come on duty on the sabbath; for Jehoiada the priest did not dismiss the divisions. ⁹And Jehoiada the priest delivered to the captains the spears and the large and small shields that had been King David's, which were in the house of God; ¹⁰and he set all the people as a guard for the king, every man with his weapon in his hand, from the south side of the house to the north side of the house, around the altar and the house. ¹¹Then he brought out the king's son, and put the crown upon him, and gave him the testimony; and they proclaimed him king, and Jehoiada and his sons anointed him, and they said, "Long live the king.". . .

¹⁶And Jehoiada made a covenant between himself and all the people and the king that they should be the Lord's people. ¹⁷Then all the people went to the house of Baal, and tore it down; his altars and his images they broke in pieces, and they slew Mattan the priest of Baal before the altars. ¹⁸And Jehoiada posted watchmen for the house of the Lord under the direction of the Levitical priests and the Levites whom David had organized to be in charge of the house of the Lord, to offer burnt offerings to the Lord, as it is written in the law of Moses, with rejoicing and with singing, according to the order of David. ¹⁹He stationed the gatekeepers at the gates of the house of the Lord so that no one should enter who was in any way unclean. ²⁰And he took the captains, the nobles, the governors of the people, and all the people of the land; and they brought the king down from the house of the Lord, marching through the upper gate to the king's house. And they set the king upon the royal throne. ²¹So all the people of the land rejoiced; and the city was quiet, after Athaliah had been slain with the sword.

One last dying flame of the house of Omri flashes up briefly in Athaliah who proves herself a true daughter of Jezebel by killing off all who might prove an opposition to her wishes (cf. 1 Kings 21). The day is saved for the house of David, however, by the action of a princess of that line, Jehoshabeath. The Chronicler makes her the wife of Jehoida the priest who is the hero of the story of the eventual downfall of Athaliah. The account differs very little from that in Kings except for the more prominent part played by priests and Levites. Jehoiada has the support of the military and all the people but since it is the priests and Levites who can enter the Temple it is they who actually carry out the coup in Chronicles.

After the coup there is covenant making. In Kings the covenant is between God and the people, the notion of corporate personality ensuring that the king represents God before the people and the people before God. But Chronicles interposes the person of the priest, Jehoiada, so it is he rather than the king who stands as representative. This reflects post-exilic times when there was no longer a king and the priesthood was more and more seen in a representative role. The terms of the covenant being that they should worship Yahweh alone (cf. 2 Chron 15:12), the result is that the worship of Baal is outlawed yet once again in the land.

KINGS WHOSE ENDS
WERE NOT IN THEIR BEGINNINGS
24:1—27:9.

Joash
24:1-27.

> **24** Joash was seven years old when he began to reign, and he reigned forty years in Jerusalem; his mother's name was Zibiah of Beer-sheba. ²And Joash did what was right in the eyes of the Lord all the days of Jehoiada the priest. ³Jehoiada got for him two wives, and he had sons and daughters.

⁴After this Joash decided to restore the house of the Lord. ⁵And he gathered the priests and the Levites, and said to them, "Go out to the cities of Judah, and gather from all Israel money to repair the house of your God from year to year; and see that you hasten the matter." But the Levites did not hasten it. ⁶So the king summoned Jehoiada the chief, and said to him, "Why have you not required the Levites to bring in from Judah and Jerusalem the tax levied by Moses, the servant of the Lord, on the congregation of Israel for the tent of testimony?" ⁷For the sons of Athaliah, that wicked woman, had broken into the house of God; and had also used all the dedicated things of the house of the Lord for the Baals.

⁸So the king commanded, and they made a chest, and set it outside the gate of the house of the Lord. . . .

¹⁵But Jehoiada grew old and full of days, and died; he was a hundred and thirty years old at his death. ¹⁶And they buried him in the city of David among the kings, because he had done good in Israel, and toward God and his house.

¹⁷Now after the death of Jehoiada the princes of Judah came and did obeisance to the king; then the king harkened to them. ¹⁸And they forsook the house of the Lord, the God of their fathers, and served the Asherim and the idols. . . .

²⁰Then the Spirit of God took possession of Zechariah the son of Jehoiada the priest; and he stood above the people, and said to them, "Thus says God, 'Why do you transgress the commandments of the Lord, so that you cannot prosper? Because you have forsaken the Lord, he has forsaken you.' " ²¹But they conspired against him, and by command of the king they stoned him with stones in the court of the house of the Lord. ²²Thus Joash the king did not remember the kindness which Jehoiada, Zechariah's father, had shown him, but killed his son. And when he was dying, he said, "May the Lord see and avenge!"

²³At the end of the year the army of the Syrians came

up against Joash. They came to Judah and Jerusalem, and destroyed all the princes of the people from among the people, and sent all their spoil to the king of Damascus. ²⁴Though the army of the Syrians had come with few men, the Lord delivered into their hand a very great army, because they had forsaken the Lord, the God of their fathers. Thus they executed judgment on Joash.

²⁵When they had departed from him, leaving him severely wounded, his servants conspired against him because of the blood of the son of Jehoiada the priest, and slew him on his bed. So he died; and they buried him in the city of David, but they did not bury him in the tombs of the kings.

Joash started off well but only, it would appear, because of the iron grip of the man who had placed him in power. Jehoiada, in obvious control, even limited the number of the king's wives to two, a number which was more in accord with the Law than the numerous wives of the earlier kings (cf. Deut 17:17). The first action of the king, no doubt spurred on by Jehoiada, was the structural repair of the Temple. The Temple had been in existence for some one hundred and thirty years by this time and this, added to the probable neglect of previous reigns, necessitated a complete overhaul. The Levites were involved in collecting the tax levied for the work and, for once, an adverse criticism is directed against them by the Chronicler in that they were lazy about getting on with the collection. The king takes the matter into his own hands and institutes what was probably the original of all church door collection boxes (24:8).

In the midst of all his zeal for the house of God one can discern a lack of heart in the young king. In speaking to the Levites he calls Yahweh, "your God." This recalls Jeremiah 42 where princes and people ask the prophet to intercede for them to the "Lord your God" and Jeremiah retorts that he is their God as much as his. There is no such rebuke recorded of Jehoiada here. Perhaps he was satisfied with externals and how external Joash's reform was, came to be seen after the priest's death. No sooner had Jehoiada been buried with all due honour than the king defects, spurred on by his princes who were probably waiting for this opportunity. Kings does not mention this defection. Either the Chronicler is using another source here (24:27), or else he feels that the king must have done wrong, given the fact of his subsequent shameful death. This would then be another example of his doctrine of retribution. The defection is followed by a denunciatory prophecy on the part of Jehoiada's son, a prophecy which provokes a violent reaction and ends in the prophet's death. The end comes quickly and relentlessly for Joash; evils from without and enemies from within lead to a shameful death and dishonourable burial.

Amaziah
25:1-28.

25 Amaziah was twenty-five years old when he began to reign, and he reigned twenty-nine years in Jerusalem. His mother's name was Jehoaddan of Jerusalem. ²And he did what was right in the eyes of the Lord, yet not with a blameless heart. ³And as soon as the royal power was firmly in his hand he killed his servants who had slain the king his father. ⁴But he did not put their children to death, according to what is written in the law, in the book of Moses, where the Lord commanded, "The fathers shall not be put to death for the children, or the children be put to death for the fathers; but every man shall die for his own sin."

⁵Then Amaziah assembled the men of Judah, and set them by fathers' houses under commanders of thousands and of hundreds for all Judah and Benjamin. He mustered those twenty years old and upward, and found that they were three hundred thousand picked men, fit for war, able to handle spear and shield. ⁶He hired also a hundred thousand mighty men of valor from Israel for a hundred talents of silver. ⁷But a man of God came to him and said, "O king, do not let the army of Israel go with you, for the Lord is not with Israel, with all the Ephra-

imites.   ⁸But if you suppose that in this way you will be
strong for war, God will cast you down before the enemy;
for God has power to help or to cast down.". . .

¹⁴After Amaziah came from the slaughter of the Edom-
ites, he brought the gods of the men of Seir, and set them
up as his gods, and worshiped them, making offerings to
them. ¹⁵Therefore the Lord was angry with Amaziah and
sent to him a prophet, who said to him, "Why have you
resorted to the gods of a people, which did not deliver
their own people from your hand?" ¹⁶But as he was
speaking the king said to him, "Have we made you a royal
counselor? Stop! Why should you be put to death?" So
the prophet stopped, but said, "I know that God has
determined to destroy you, because you have done this
and have not listened to my counsel."

¹⁷Then Amaziah king of Judah took counsel and sent
to Joash the son of Jehoahaz, son of Jehu, king of Israel,
saying, "Come, let us look one another in the face." ¹⁸And
Joash the king of Israel sent word to Amaziah king of
Judah, "A thistle on Lebanon sent to a cedar on
Lebanon, saying, 'Give your daughter to my son for a
wife'; and a wild beast of Lebanon passed by and
trampled down the thistle. ¹⁹You say, 'See, I have smitten
Edom,' and your heart has lifted you up in boastfulness.
But now stay at home; why should you provoke trouble
so that you fall, you and Judah with you?"

²⁰But Amaziah would not listen; for it was of God, in
order that he might give them into the hand of their
enemies, because they had sought the gods of Edom. ²¹So
Joash king of Israel went up; and he and Amaziah king of
Judah faced one another in battle at Bethshemesh, which
belongs to Judah. ²³And Judah was defeated by Israel,
and every man fled to his home. . . .

²⁵Amaziah the son of Joash king of Judah lived fifteen
years after the death of Joash the son of Jehoahaz, king of
Israel. ²⁶Now the rest of the deeds of Amaziah, from first
to last, are they not written in the Book of the Kings of
Judah and Israel? ²⁷From the time when he turned away

from the Lord they made a conspiracy against him in Jerusalem, and he fled to Lachish. But they sent after him to Lachish, and slew him there. 28And they brought him upon horses; and he was buried with his fathers in the city of David.

Amaziah also starts off well and is considered a good king by the Chronicler's source in Kings but, like Joash before him, he dies a violent and shameful death. Therefore, for the Chronicler, he must have done wrong. He finds this wrong chiefly in his dealings with the North but also adds that he worshipped the gods of the people he conquered in battle (vv.14-16).

Amaziah tried to continue the friendly relations with the northern monarchy which had existed earlier. He began by hiring from among the northern people mercenaries for his army. This is utterly condemned by a prophet who states categorically that "the Lord is not with Israel" (v.7). This stems from the fact that they are still in a state of rebellion against God through the apostasy of their kings down the ages (see comment on chapters ten and thirteen). Their involvement in an enterprise would doom it to failure from the start. Amaziah wins his battle without their help and, full of pride, he tries to take on Joash of Israel. The latter, in his answer, makes use of a favourite image for a parable: the comparison between a cedar in Lebanon and some lowly tree or shrub which exalts itself against the cedar to its own ruin (cf. Judg 9:7-15). So, in his pride, Amaziah brings about his own ruin and ends his days as a hunted man.

Uzziah and Jotham
26:1—27:9.

26 And all the people of Judah took Uzziah, who was sixteen years old, and made him king instead of his father Amaziah. 2He built Eloth and restored it to Judah, after the king slept with his fathers. 3Uzziah was sixteen years old when he began to reign, and he reigned fifty-two years in Jerusalem. His mother's name was Jecoliah of Jerusa-

lem. ⁴And he did what was right in the eyes of the Lord, according to all that his father Amaziah had done. ⁵He set himself to seek God in the days of Zechariah, who instructed him in the fear of God; and as long as he sought the Lord, God made him prosper.

⁶He went out and made war against the Philistines, and broke down the wall of Gath and the wall of Jabneh and the wall of Ashdod; and he built cities in the territory of Ashdod and elsewhere among the Philistines. ⁷God helped him against the Philistines, and against the Arabs that dwelt in Gurbaal, and against the Meunites. ⁸The Ammonites paid tribute to Uzziah, and his fame spread even to the border of Egypt, for he became very strong. ⁹Moreover Uzziah built towers in Jerusalem at the Corner Gate and at the Valley Gate and at the Angle, and fortified them. ¹⁰And he built towers in the wilderness, and hewed out many cisterns, for he had large herds, both in the Shephelah and in the plain, and he had farmers and vinedressers in the hills and in the fertile lands, for he loved the soil. . . .

¹⁴And Uzziah prepared for all the army shields, spears, helmets, coats of mail, bows, and stones for slinging. ¹⁵In Jerusalem he made engines, invented by skilful men, to be on the towers and the corners, to shoot arrows and great stones. And his fame spread far, for he was marvelously helped, till he was strong.

¹⁶But when he was strong he grew proud, to his destruction. For he was false to the Lord his God, and entered the temple of the Lord to burn incense on the altar of incense. ¹⁷But Azariah the priest went in after him, with eighty priests of the Lord who were men of valor; ¹⁸and they withstood King Uzziah, and said to him, "It is not for you, Uzziah, to burn incense to the Lord, but for the priests the sons of Aaron, who are consecrated to burn incense. Go out of the sanctuary; for you have done wrong, and it will bring you no honor from the Lord God." ¹⁹Then Uzziah was angry. Now he had a censer in his hand to burn incense, and when he became angry with the

priests leprosy broke out on his forehead, in the presence of the priests in the house of the Lord, by the altar of incense. [20]And Azariah the chief priest, and all the priests, looked at him, and behold, he was leprous in his forehead! And they thrust him out quickly, and he himself hastened to go out, because the Lord had smitten him. [21]And King Uzziah was a leper to the day of his death, and being a leper dwelt in a separate house, for he was excluded from the house of the Lord. And Jotham his son was over the king's household, governing the people of the land

[22]Now the rest of the acts of Uzziah, from first to last, Isaiah the prophet the son of Amoz wrote. [23]And Uzziah slept with his fathers, and they buried him with his fathers in the burial field which belonged to the kings, for they said, "He is a leper." And Jotham his son reigned in his stead.

27 Jotham was twenty-five years old when he began to reign, and he reigned sixteen years in Jerusalem. His mother's name was Jerushah the daughter of Zadok. [2]And he did what was right in the eyes of the Lord according to all that his father Uzziah had done—only he did not invade the temple of the Lord. But the people still followed corrupt practices. [3]He built the upper gate of the house of the Lord, and did much building on the wall of Ophel.

Uzziah was one of the most politically powerful in the succession of Davidic kings. His expansionist activities, his care for building, agriculture, his military strength, all come through in the concise account of his reign in Chronicles and is borne out by archaeological finds. In particular his care for agriculture has been well demonstrated by excavations in the Negev near Beersheba where remains of forts, draining systems, cisterns and farms can be dated to his time. Likewise his building activities have been authenticated, for example in Eloth, the Ezion-geber of Solomon's time, near modern Elath. A seal was found in the excavations there bearing the inscription: "(belonging) to Jotham," more than likely Jotham, the son of Uzziah, who ruled as co-regent in the latter days of his father.

The activity of the king was also to be seen in the provision of arms for his soldiers (vv. 14-15) who no longer supplied their own but got them from the king. This resulted in increased efficiency and inventiveness. Some commentators would see in the "engines invented by skillful men" a mention of catapults to fire large stones and, since these were probably not invented until 400 B.C. (possibly in Syracuse), this fact has been used to date Chronicles to a much later time, since it would have taken some time for such inventions to travel as far as Judah. But what is in question here is probably defensive constructions on the walls of a city which enabled soldiers to shoot from behind in comparative safety. Such constructions can be seen in Assyrian reliefs of the siege of Lachish which took place some fifty or so years after this time and so could have easily been in use already in the time of Uzziah.

But this very successful man died a leper and so the Chronicler, as always, has to find a reason for this ignominious end (see Intro. p. 8). He finds it in the pride which makes the king usurp priestly duties (cf. Num 16). It is interesting to note that when the priest, Azariah, is rebuking the king for his attempt to offer incense, a duty by this time reserved to the priests but which in earlier times could be offered by royalty, he does not give him his kingly title but merely calls him "Uzziah." The king's leprosy was the reason for his son's co-regency as it must have been of such a kind as to prevent him from fulfilling official duties. Nothing much of note is recorded of Jotham's reign except for his building activities. The mention of Isaiah as writing the acts of Uzziah links us to the great prophet of the eighth century who records that his inaugural vision took place "in the year that King Uzziah died" (Is 6:1) and whose oracles are dated "in the days of Uzziah, Jotham, Ahaz and Hezekiah, kings of Judah" (Is 1:1).

A KING WHO DID NOTHING RIGHT
28:1-27.

Ahaz
28:1-27.

28 Ahaz was twenty years old when he began to reign, and he reigned sixteen years in Jerusalem. And he did not do what was right in the eyes of the Lord, like his father David, ²but walked in the ways of the kings of Israel. He even made molten images for the Baals; ³and he burned incense in the valley of the son of Hinnom, and burned his sons as an offering, according to the abominable practices of the nations whom the Lord drove out before the people of Israel. ⁴And he sacrificed and burned incense on the high places, and on the hills, and under every green tree.

⁵Therefore the Lord his God gave him into the hand of the king of Syria, who defeated him and took captive a great number of his people and brought them to Damascus. He was also given into the hand of the king of Israel, who defeated him with great slaughter. . . .

⁸The men of Israel took captive two hundred thousand of their kinsfolk, women, sons, and daughters; they also took much spoil from them and brought the spoil to Samaria. ⁹But a prophet of the Lord was there, whose name was Obed; and he went out to meet the army that came to Samaria, and said to them, "Behold, because the Lord, the God of your fathers, was angry with Judah, he gave them into your hand, but you have slain them in a rage which has reached up to heaven. ¹⁰And now you intend to subjugate the people of Judah and Jerusalem, male and female, as your slaves. Have you not sins of your own against the Lord your God? ¹¹Now hear me, and send back the captives from your kinsfolk whom you have taken, for the fierce wrath of the Lord is upon you.". . .

¹⁴So the armed men left the captives and the spoil before the princes and all the assembly. ¹⁵And the men

who have been mentioned by name rose and took the captives, and with the spoil they clothed all that were naked among them; they clothed them, gave them sandals, provided them with food and drink, and anointed them; and carrying all the feeble among them on asses, they brought them to their kinsfolk at Jericho, the city of palm trees. Then they returned to Samaria.

[16]At that time King Ahaz sent to the king of Assyria for help. [17]For the Edomites had again invaded and defeated Judah, and carried away captives. [18]And the Philistines had made raids on the cities in the Shephelah and the Negeb of Judah, and had taken Bethshemesh, Aijalon, Gederoth, Soco with its villages, Timnah with its villages, and Gimzo with its villages; and they settled there. [19]For the Lord brought Judah low because of Ahaz king of Israel, for he had dealt wantonly in Judah and had been faithless to the Lord. [20]So Tilgathpilneser king of Assyria came against him. and afflicted him instead of strengthening him. [21]For Ahaz took from the house of the Lord and the house of the king and of the princes, and gave tribute to the king of Assyria; but it did not help him.

[22]In the time of his distress he became yet more faithless to the Lord—this same King Ahaz. [23]For he sacrificed to the gods of Damascus which had defeated him, and said, "Because the gods of the kings of Syria helped them, I will sacrifice to them that they may help me." But they were the ruin of him, and of all Israel. [24]And Ahaz gathered together the vessels of the house of God and cut in pieces the vessels of the house of God, and he shut up the doors of the house of the Lord; and he made himself altars in every corner of Jerusalem. [25]In every city of Judah he made high places to burn incense to other gods, provoking to anger the Lord, the God of his fathers. [26]Now the rest of his acts and all his ways, from first to last, behold, they are written in the Book of the Kings of Judah and Israel. [27]And Ahaz slept with his fathers, and they buried him in the city, in Jerusalem, for they did not bring him

into the tombs of the kings of Israel. And Hezekiah his son reigned in his stead.

This section of Chronicles ends as it began with a state of rebellion and apostasy (cf. 2 Chron 10-13) only this time it is Judah which appears as totally given over to the worship of false gods and, therefore, to total political collapse. The end, as far as the Chronicler is concerned, comes with his statement that Ahaz "shut up the doors of the house of the Lord," the very Temple on which the South depended for its legitimacy. The picture is not quite so bleak in the parallel section of Kings (cf. 2 Kings 16) though the portrait of Ahaz in Isaiah (Is 7-9) resembles that of Chronicles and, therefore, bids fair to be authentic. It seems probable that the deliberate intention of the Chronicler is to portray Ahaz as committing the very sins which the northern kings were accused of when they refused to return from their apostasy (cf. 2 Chron 13) and by that very fact the South was now also seen to be in a state of apostasy.

In a deliberate contrast to his picture of Ahaz, the Chronicler now portrays Northerners in a favourable light. They listen to the word of a prophet, prove "kinsfolk" to the defeated Judeans and send them home clad and well-fed. Above all, they acknowledge their past guilt and do not add to it by taking advantage of their kinsfolk's distress. Significantly, it is not the northern king who instigates such noble actions but "certain chiefs" of the people. The kingship in Israel remains apostate in face of the final breakup of the kingdom when Samaria was captured and many led off into exile (2 Kings 17), but the Chronicler is pointing perhaps to a faithful remnant among the people of the North who really are part of the true Israel (see Intro. p. 7). They will reappear in subsequent chapters.

Ahaz rushes headlong into destruction by his doubtful political sense in appealing for help to Assyria rather than depending on God (cf. Is 7). His distress does not bring about repentance and this to the Chronicler is the ultimate sin, enough to refuse him burial in the tombs of the kings.

Ahaz, therefore, is the epitome of all that a king should not be as already portrayed in the person of Saul and subsequently lived out by so many of the kings of Judah. But the end is not yet; just as David and Solomon followed Saul, so a new Davidic king will arise to cleanse the Temple and renew the land.

RESTORATION AND COLLAPSE
29:1—36:23

Hezekiah's Reform
29:1—31:21.

29 Hezekiah began to reign when he was twenty-five years old, and he reigned twenty-nine years in Jerusalem. His mother's name was Abijah the daughter of Zechariah. 2And he did what was right in the eyes of the Lord, according to all that David his father had done.

3In the first year of his reign, in the first month, he opened the doors of the house of the Lord and repaired them. . . .

20Then Hezekiah the king rose early and gathered the officials of the city, and went up to the house of the Lord. 21And they brought seven bulls, seven rams, seven lambs, and seven he-goats for a sin offering for the kingdom and for the sanctuary and for Judah. And he commanded the priests the sons of Aaron to offer them on the altar of the Lord. 22So they killed the bulls, and the priests received the blood and threw it against the altar; and they killed the rams and their blood was thrown against the altar; and they killed the lambs and their blood was thrown against the altar. 23Then the he-goats for the sin offering were brought to the king and the assembly, and they laid their hands upon them, 24and the priests killed them and made a sin offering with their blood on the altar, to make atonement for all Israel. For the king commanded that the burnt offering and the sin offering should be made for all Israel. . . .

30And Hezekiah the king and the princes commanded the Levites to sing praises to the Lord with the words of David and of Asaph the seer. And they sang praises with gladness, and they bowed down and worshiped. . . .

34But the priests were too few and could not flay all the burnt offerings, so until other priests had sanctified themselves their brethren the Levites helped them, until the work was finished—for the Levites were more upright in heart than the priests in sanctifying themselves. 35Besides the great number of burnt offerings there was the fat of the peace offerings, and there were the libations for the burnt offerings. Thus the service of the house of the Lord was restored. 36And Hezekiah and all the people rejoiced because of what God had done for the people; for the thing came about suddenly.

During the reigns of David and Solomon Israel had been a fully united nation. The subsequent division of the kingdom had lasted for three hundred years and ended in total failure: the collapse of the northern kingdom and the total breakdown in religious and civil life in the South. With the coming of a new king in Judah who was faithful to God, the Chronicler envisages a new era beginning, not just for those in the South but for all God's people who formed the one Israel (see Intro. p. 7). Now that the illegitimate kingship was about to disappear in the North, there was much less to stand in the way of a return to one united Israel centred on Jerusalem. The whole nation could come into a new relationship with God by renewing its covenant obligations (cf. Ezek 37). The lesson for the Chronicler's time is obvious: it is in the unity forged by gathering around the Temple in Jerusalem that the people's strength will lie.

The first step towards the realisation of that ideal was the purification of the Temple which had been defiled by Ahaz.

The Chronicler has Hezekiah set about this task as early as possible in his reign. The Levites are prominent in the task of purification, unlike the priests who seemed slow to rally round, possibly, it has been suggested by some commentators, because they themselves had participated in Ahab's apostasy. The functions of the Levites are extended and Hezekiah is said to have depended on their loyalty at every stage of the endeavour.

The Temple is cleansed in record time and a great celebration follows in which the cymbals, harps, lyres and trumpets are again to be heard. Praises are sung in the words of David and Asaph, the seer. It is probable that this reflects an actual hymnal or psalter already in use in the time of the Chronicler.

The Passover
30:1-27.

30 Hezekiah sent to all Israel and Judah, and wrote letters also to Ephraim and Manasseh, that they should come to the house of the Lord at Jerusalem, to keep the passover to the Lord the God of Israel. ²For the king and his princes and all the assembly in Jerusalem had taken counsel to keep the passover in the second month—³for they could not keep it in its time because the priests had not sanctified themselves in sufficient number, nor had the people assembled in Jerusalem—⁴and the plan seemed right to the king and all the assembly. ⁵So they decreed to make a proclamation throughout all Israel, from Beersheba to Dan, that the people should come and keep the passover to the Lord the God of Israel, at Jerusalem; for they had not kept it in great numbers as prescribed. ⁶So couriers went throughout all Israel and Judah with letters from the king and his princes, as the king had commanded, saying, "O people of Israel, return to the Lord, the God of Abraham, Isaac, and Israel, that he may turn again to the remnant of you who have escaped from the hand of the kings of Assyria. ⁷Do not be like your fathers and your brethren, who were faithless to the Lord God of their fathers, so that he made them a desolation, as you see. [8]Do not now be stiff-necked as your fathers were, but yield yourselves to the Lord, and come to his sanctuary, which he has sanctified for ever, and serve the Lord your God, that his fierce anger may turn away from you. [9]For if you return to the Lord, your brethren and your children will find compassion with their captors, and return to this land. For the Lord your God is gracious and merciful, and will not turn away his face from you, if you return to him.". . .

[13]And many people came together in Jerusalem to keep the feast of unleavened bread in the second month, a very great assembly. . . .

[23]Then the whole assembly agreed together to keep the feast for another seven days; so they kept it for another seven days with gladness. [24]For Hezekiah king of Judah gave the assembly a thousand bulls and seven thousand sheep for offerings, and the princes gave the assembly a thousand bulls and ten thousand sheep. And the priests sanctified themselves in great numbers. [25]The whole assembly of Judah, and the priests and the Levites, and the whole assembly that came out of Israel, and the sojourners who came out of the land of Israel, and the sojourners who dwelt in Judah, rejoiced.

The next step in welding the people into a unity around the sanctuary was to hold a great Passover, the feast which celebrated the liberation of the people from Egypt. Since the days of Jeroboam, the North had kept the Passover at a different date from the South (1 Kings 12:32) and there may be the implication here that Hezekiah was trying to accommodate the North. As well as this the cleansing of the Temple had not finished in time for the Passover to take place in the first month, therefore a law in the Pentateuch (Num 9:9-12) is availed of to allow it to take place in the second month. A circular letter is written to "all Israel from Beersheba to Dan" (which was the traditional description of the whole land). The letter is in the form of the levitical sermon, a form noted so often on the mouth of prophets in earlier chapters and is a portrayal of the Chronicler's theology that those who return to the Lord find peace and consolation.

There is no mention of this appeal to the North in Kings and, historically, it would be difficult to place it so early in the reign of Hezekiah because the North only fell to Assyria in the sixth year of his reign (2 Kings 18:10). This then is an idealisation of the Chronicler and it shows once again his concern to include all the people of Israel in any scheme of restoration and renewal centred around the Temple.

It is obvious from his description of Hezekiah that the Chronicler sees him as another Solomon. The land is regarded as a whole again, as in Solomon's time, with all its people able to come to Jerusalem for the Passover. The feast marking the completion of the Temple lasted two weeks in Solomon's time. So also at the end of the restoration by Hezekiah. The order of that restoration (29:18) follows the pattern for Temple worship outlined originally by Solomon (2:4). Also parallel is the outstanding wealth of both kings (32:27-29; cf. 9:13) as is the attitude of gentile nations to them (32:23; cf. 9:1-28). The Chronicler makes the parallel explicit when he observes at the end of the Passover celebration: "So there was great joy in Jerusalem, for since the time of Solomon the son of David king of Israel there had been nothing like this in Jerusalem" (30:26).

Since Solomon was the pattern of the ideal king, Hezekiah can be considered his most outstanding successor. This honour was reserved for Josiah in Kings where, as has been noted, any mention of reform was avoided until his time. The Chronicler may be more accurate here since if Ahaz was even half as lax as he is portrayed to be, there certainly would have been need for some cleaning up in his wake. The portrayal of Hezekiah, then, in the different works is another example of the historical methods used in them. Only what is needed for the instruction of the people addressed is highlighted in any given period.

Other Activities of Hezekiah
31:1—32:33

31 Now when all this was finished, all Israel who were present went out to the cities of Judah and broke in pieces the pillars and hewed down the Asherim and broke down the high places and the altars throughout all Judah and Benjamin, and in Ephraim and Manasseh, until they had destroyed them all. Then all the people of Israel returned to their cities, every man to his possession.

²And Hezekiah appointed the divisions of the priests and of the Levites, division by division, each according to his service, the priests and the Levites, for burnt offerings and peace offerings, to minister in the gates of the camp of the Lord and to give thanks and praise. ³The contribution of the king from his own possessions was for the burnt offerings: the burnt offerings of morning and evening, and the burnt offerings for the sabbaths, the new moons, and the appointed feasts, as it is written in the law of the Lord. ⁴And he commanded the people who lived in Jerusalem to give the portion due to the priests and the Levites, that they might give themselves to the law of the Lord. ⁵As soon as the command was spread abroad, the people of Israel gave in abundance the first fruits of grain, wine, oil, honey, and of all the produce of the field; and they brought in abundantly the tithe of everything. ⁶And the people of Israel and Judah who lived in the cities of Judah also brought in the tithe of cattle and sheep, and the dedicated things which had been consecrated to the Lord their God, and laid them in heaps. . . .

²⁰Thus Hezekiah did throughout all Judah; and he did what was good and right and faithful before the Lord his God. ²¹And every work that he undertook in the service of the house of God and in accordance with the law and the commandments, seeking his God, he did with all his heart, and prospered.

32 After these things and these acts of faithfulness Sennacherib king of Assyria came and invaded Judah and encamped against the fortified cities, thinking to win them for himself. ²And when Hezekiah saw that Sennacherib had come and intended to fight against Jerusalem, ³he planned with his officers and his mighty men to stop the water of the springs that were outside the city; and they helped him. ⁴A great many people were gathered, and they stopped all the springs and the brook that flowed through the land, saying, "Why should the kings of Assyria come and find much water?" ⁵He set to work resolutely and built up all the wall that was broken down, and raised towers upon it, and outside it he built another wall; and he strengthened the Millo in the city of David. He also made weapons and shields in abundance. ⁶And he set combat commanders over the people, and gathered them together to him in the square at the gate of the city and spoke encouragingly to them, saying, ⁷"Be strong and of good courage. Do not be afraid or dismayed before the king of Assyria and all the horde that is with him; for there is one greater with us than with him. ⁸With him is an arm of flesh; but with us is the Lord our God, to help us and to fight out battles." And the people took confidence from the words of Hezekiah king of Judah. . . .

²⁰Then Hezekiah the king and Isaiah the prophet, the son of Amoz, prayed because of this and cried to heaven. ²¹And the Lord sent an angel, who cut off all the mighty warriors and commanders and officers in the camp of the king of Assyria. So he returned with shame of face to his own land. And when he came into the house of his god, some of his own sons struck him down there with the sword. ²²So the Lord saved Hezekiah and the inhabitants of Jerusalem from the hand of Sennacherib king of Assyria and from the hand of all his enemies; and he gave them rest on every side. ²³And many brought gifts to the Lord to Jerusalem and precious things to Hezekiah king of Judah, so that he was exalted in the sight of all nations from that time onward.

²⁴In those days Hezekiah became sick and was at the point of death, and he prayed to the Lord; and he answered him and gave him a sign. ²⁵But Hezekiah did not

make return according to the benefit done to him, for his heart was proud. Therefore wrath came upon him and Judah and Jerusalem. ²⁶But Hezekiah humbled himself for the pride of his heart, both he and the inhabitants of Jerusalem, so that the wrath of the Lord did not come upon them in the days of Hezekiah.

A description follows of the mopping-up operations throughout the remainder of the land and of the consolidation of Temple arrangements before the Chronicler finally arrives at the more secular activity of Hezekiah. Little appears in these chapters of the intense military and political activity in which Hezekiah engaged almost throughout the whole of his career in his capacity as head of the anti-Assyrian league. The account of his deliverance from the Assyrian army under Sennacherib (2 Kings 19) is abbreviated to bring out the Chronicler's essential point that devout prayer can change a situation radically because God is with those who have a sincere heart.

The prophet, Isaiah was associated with Hezekiah in his prayer for the deliverance of Jerusalem at this time (32:20) but much of the interaction between king and prophet at this stage is missing (cf. Is 37:14-35) as is that between them on the king's subsequent illness (Is 38). Here also the essential point is made: Hezekiah prayed to the Lord and he answered him (32:24). What was probably the greatest achievement of Hezekiah, the rechannelling of water into the city by means of an underground tunnel, only merits one verse (32:30). A witness to this great feat of engineering remains to this day in the shape of an inscription which was found in the tunnel, placed where the two teams of workmen boring from either side eventually met in the middle. It reads: "(the completing of) the piercing through. And this is the story of the piercing through. While (the stone-cutters were swinging their) axes, each towards his fellow, and while there were yet three cubits to be pierced through, (there was heard) the voice of a man calling to his fellow, for there was a crevice on the right . . . and on the day of the piercing through, the stone-cutters struck through each to meet his fellow, axe against axe. Then ran the water from **the Spring** to the Pool for twelve hundred cubits, and a hundred cubits was the height of the rock above the head of the stone-cutters."

Manasseh and Amon
33:1-25.

33 Manasseh was twelve years old when he began to reign, and he reigned fifty-five years in Jerusalem. [2]He did what was evil in the sight of the Lord, according to the abominable practices of the nations whom the Lord drove out before the people of Israel. [3]For he rebuilt the high places which his father Hezekiah had broken down, and erected altars to the Baals, and made Asherahs, and worshiped all the host of heaven, and served them. . . .

[10]The Lord spoke to Manasseh and to his people, but they gave no heed. [11]Therefore the Lord brought upon them the commanders of the army of the king of Assyria, who took Manasseh with hooks and bound him with fetters of bronze and brought him to Babylon. [12]And when he was in distress he entreated the favor of the Lord his God and humbled himself greatly before the God of his fathers. [13]He prayed to him, and God received his entreaty and heard his supplication and brought him again to Jerusalem into his kingdom. Then Manasseh knew that the Lord was God.

[14]Afterwards he built an outer wall for the city of David west of Gihon, in the valley, and for the entrance into the Fish Gate, and carried it round Ophel, and raised it to a very great height; he also put commanders of the army in all the fortified cities in Judah. [15]And he took away the foreign gods and the idol from the house of the Lord, and all the altars that he had built on the mountain of the house of the Lord and in Jerusalem, and he threw them outside of the city. [16]He also restored the altar of the Lord

and offered upon it sacrifices of peace offerings and of thanksgiving; and he commanded Judah to serve the Lord the God of Israel. [17]Nevertheless the people still sacrificed at the high places, but only to the Lord their God.

[18]Now the rest of the acts of Manasseh, and his prayer to his God, and the words of the seers who spoke to him in the name of the Lord the God of Israel, behold, they are in the Chronicles of the Kings of Israel. [19]And his prayer, and how God received his entreaty, and all his sin and his faithlessness, and the sites on which he built high places and set up the Asherim and the images, before he humbled himself, behold, they are written in the Chronicles of the Seers. [20]So Manasseh slept with his fathers, and they buried him in his house; and Amon his son reigned in his stead.

[21]Amon was twenty-two years old when he began to reign, and he reigned two years in Jerusalem. [22]He did what was evil in the sight of the Lord, as Manasseh his father had done. Amon sacrificed to all the images that Manasseh his father had made, and served them. [23]And he did not humble himself before the Lord, as Manasseh his father had humbled himself, but this Amon incurred guilt more and more. [24]And his servants conspired against him and killed him in his house. [25]But the people of the land slew all those who had conspired against King Amon; and the people of the land made Josiah his son king in his stead.

Hezekiah's reform was short-lived. Perhaps this was the reason why Kings paid little heed to it. But in accordance with the Chronicler's theory of individual retribution, each reign has to be judged separately. That is why he had quite a problem with Manasseh. How could a king who had done every evil in the Chronicler's book possibly have been so prosperous and have had such a long life? Long life and prosperity being the highest of rewards, there was only one explanation possible: he must have repented at some stage of his life. Kings says, no, he was always bad and the prophet Jeremiah agrees (Jer 15:4). Kings knows nothing of a trip to Assyria which according to the Chronicler could have changed his mind. Confirmatory evidence for this trip is found on a cylinder of King Esarhaddon on which the name of Manasseh appears on a list of vassal kings who appeared before their master to pay tribute to him. There is no mention of his being bound in "fetters of bronze" (33:11), so the Chronicler has his own interpretation of the trip. He solves his problem of retribution by presuming that Manasseh got such a fright in Assyria that he repented and did good for the remainder of his long life.

The contrary evidence remains in the text, however, since in the record of Manasseh's son, Amon, it is written that he walked according to the wicked ways of his father with no account being taken of the latter's repentance. The tradition of this repentance survived in the form of a beautiful "Prayer of Manasseh" which was probably only composed just before the time of Christ. It is included among the Apographa in Protestant Bibles and was given as an appendix to 2 Maccabees in the Douay Bible.

Josiah's Reform
34:1—35:27.

34 Josiah was eight years old when he began to reign, and he reigned thirty-one years in Jerusalem. ²He did what was right in the eyes of the Lord, and walked in the ways of David his father; and he did not turn aside to the right or to the left. ³For in the eighth year of his reign, while he was yet a boy, he began to seek the God of David his father; and in the twelfth year he began to purge Judah and Jerusalem of the high places, the Asherim, and the graven and the molten images. . . .

⁸Now in the eighteenth year of his reign, when he had purged the land and the house, he sent Shaphan the son of Azaliah, and Maaseiah the governor of the city, and

Joah the son of Joahaz, the recorder, to repair the house of the Lord his God. . . .

14While they were bringing out the money that had been brought into the house of the Lord, Hilkiah the priest found the book of the law of the Lord given through Moses. 15Then Hilkiah said to Shaphan the secretary, "I have found the book of the law in the house of the Lord"; and Hilkiah gave the book to Shaphan. 16Shaphan brought the book to the king, and further reported to the king. "All that was committed to your servants they are doing. 17They have emptied out the money that was found in the house of the Lord and have delivered it into the hand of the overseers and the workmen." 18Then Shaphan the secretary told the king, "Hilkiah the priest has given me a book." And Shaphan read it before the king.

19When the king heard the words of the law he rent his clothes. 20And the king commanded Hilkiah, Ahikam the son of Shaphan, Abdon the son of Micah, Shaphan the secretary, and Asaiah the king's servant, saying, 21"Go, inquire of the Lord for me and for those who are left in Israel and in Judah, concerning the words of the book that has been found; for great is the wrath of the Lord that is poured out on us, because our fathers have not kept the word of the Lord, to do according to all that is written in this book."

22So Hilkiah and those whom the king had sent went to Huldah the prophetess, the wife of Shallum the son of Tokhath, son of Hasrah, keeper of the wardrobe (now she dwelt in Jerusalem in the Second Quarter) and spoke to her to that effect. 23And she said to them, "Thus says the Lord, the God of Israel: 'Tell the man who sent you to me, 24Thus says the Lord, Behold, I will bring evil upon this place and upon its inhabitants, all the curses that are written in the book which was read before the king of Judah. . . .

26But to the king of Judah, who sent you to inquire of the Lord, thus shall you say to him, Thus says the Lord,

the God of Israel: Regarding the words which you
have heard, ²⁷because your heart was penitent and you
humbled yourself before God when you heard his words
against this place and its inhabitants, and you have
humbled yourself before me, and have rent your clothes
and wept before me, I also have heard you, says the Lord.
²⁸Behold, I will gather you to your fathers, and you shall
be gathered to your grave in peace, and your eyes shall
not see all the evil which I will bring upon this place and
its inhabitants.' " And they brought back word to the
king.

At the beginning of Josiah's reign, Judah was politically
as subject to Assyria as it had been during the reign of
Manasseh. Political subjugation often involved the worship
of the overlord's gods and this certainly was an element in
Manasseh's apostasy. The gradual decline in Assyria's
power enabled Josiah to cautiously reassert his independence and the return to the old religion was as much a sign of
political revolt as of religious fervour. His first step was
the reform of Jerusalem and of Judah, then he extended his
concern northwards into the territory of the former northern kingdom which had been under Assyrian rule. Getting
rid of the high places and cult centres here probably
involved the overthrow of the shrine of Bethel which had
been a threat to Jerusalem ever since the early days of the
division between the North and the South (1 Kings 12:26-
33).

Six years later Josiah began a reconstruction of the Temple and "all Israel" was again involved in its being renewed
as the true centre of worship for the entire nation. In the
course of the work, a book of the "Law of the Lord" was
found which moved the king profoundly. There has been
much controversy and speculation as to what the authors of
Kings considered the contents of this book, but it seems
clear enough that for the Chronicler it was the Pentateuch.
Spurred on by its call for repentance, the king leads the
people in a renewal of their covenant with God.

Advice is sought from a prophetess who foretells the judgment that will come on the people because of their lack of faith in God, though she asserts that Josiah will be spared on account of his repentance. It is interesting to note that this prophecy was preserved even though in actual fact Josiah was tragically killed in battle at the height of his career. The Chronicler, seeking a reason for his early death, in accordance with his theory of individual retribution (see Intro. p. 7), found it in the fact that he was disobedient to another word from God. Understandably, Josiah does not heed this word since it came through the mouth of his archenemy, Pharaoh Neco of Egypt (35:21). But, in the view of the Chronicler, God can use anyone, even so unlikely a source, as his mouthpiece.

Josiah's Passover
35:1-27.

35 Josiah kept a passover to the Lord in Jerusalem; and they killed the passover lamb on the fourteenth day of the first month. ²He appointed the priests to their offices and encouraged them in the service of the house of the Lord. ³And he said to the Levites who taught all Israel and who were holy to the Lord, "Put the holy ark in the house which Solomon the son of David, king of Israel, built; you need no longer carry it upon your shoulders. Now serve the Lord your God and his people Israel. ⁴Prepare yourselves according to your fathers' houses by your divisions, following the directions of David king of Israel and the directions of Solomon his son. . . .

⁷Then Josiah contributed to the lay people, as passover offerings for all that were present, lambs and kids from the flock to the number of thirty thousand, and three thousand bulls; these were from the king's possessions. . . .

¹⁶So all the service of the Lord was prepared that day, to keep the passover and to offer burnt offerings on the altar of the Lord, according to the command of King Josiah. ¹⁷And the people of Israel who were present kept the passover at that time, and the feast of unleavened

bread seven days. [18]No passover like it had been kept in Israel since the days of Samuel the prophet; none of the kings of Israel had kept such a passover as was kept by Josiah, and the priests and the Levites, and all Judah and Israel who were present, and the inhabitants of Jerusalem. [19]In the eighteenth year of the reign of Josiah this passover was kept.

[20]After all this, when Josiah had prepared the temple, Neco king of Egypt went up to fight at Carchemish on the Euphrates and Josiah went out against him. [21]But he sent envoys to him, saying, "What have we to do with each other, king of Judah? I am not coming against you this day, but against the house with which I am at war; and God has commanded me to make haste. Cease opposing God, who is with me, lest he destroy you." [22]Nevertheless Josiah would not turn away from him, but disguised himself in order to fight with him. He did not listen to the words of Neco from the mouth of God, but joined battle in the plain of Megiddo. [23]And the archers shot King Josiah; and the king said to his servants, "Take me away, for I am badly wounded." [24]So his servants took him out of the chariot and carried him in his second chariot and brought him to Jerusalem. And he died, and was buried in the tombs of his fathers. All Judah and Jerusalem mourned for Josiah. [25]Jeremiah also uttered a lament for Josiah; and all the singing men and singing women have spoken of Josiah in their laments to this day. They made these an ordinance in Israel; behold, they are written in the Laments. [26]Now the rest of the acts of Josiah, and his good deeds according to what is written in the law of the Lord, [27]and his acts, first and last, behold, they are written in the Book of the Kings of Israel and Judah.

This chapter begins with a notice of Josiah's great passover: "Josiah kept a passover," a notice which gives an example of corporate personality where the king sums up in himself the action of the people. As in the account of Hezekiah's passover, the appointment and encouragement of the priests and Levites is mentioned first. The section sums up the various duties of the Levites: teaching, carrying the Ark (a function which needed no longer to be exercised), killing and preparing the beasts for sacrifice. This latter duty had been an emergency function in the time of Hezekiah but now is considered a normal part of the Levites' duties. One has the impression of their ubiquitous presence; that, in fact, things could not have gone on without them.

The king provided beasts for sacrifice at his own expense. Such a provision was earlier implied of David (1 Chron 29:2-5) and of Hezekiah (2 Chron 30:24). Again the presence of the whole people is stressed and the tradition remained strong that no passover like it had been kept in Israel since early tribal days.

We know little of Josiah's other activities but they must have been considerable since it is clear that he had established his authority as far north as Megiddo (he built a large fortress there) and south into Philistia. But this expansion was cut short by his untimely death. It is probable that Pharaoh Neco of Egypt was on his way northward to assist the Assyrians whose empire was breaking up at the time. Josiah's was a last spurt of independence on the part of Judah. In Kings, the early death of Josiah is interpreted as a blessing for him personally because of his goodness. What the Chronicler thought of it has already been outlined. Again the difference in outlook is striking. There is no record of a lament for Josiah written by the prophet Jeremiah, but memory of it must have remained long after his death to have merited mention here.

Last Kings of Judah
36:1-23

36 The people of the land took Jehoahaz the son of Josiah and made him king in his father's stead in Jerusalem. ²Jehoahaz was twenty-three years old when he began to reign; and he reigned three months in Jerusalem. ³Then the king of Egypt deposed him in Jerusalem and laid upon the land a tribute of a hundred talents of silver and a talent of gold. [4]And the king of Egypt made Eliakim his brother king over Judah and Jerusalem, and changed his name to Jehoiakim; but Neco took Jehoahaz his brother and carried him to Egypt.

[5]Jehoiakim was twenty-five years old when he began to reign, and he reigned eleven years in Jerusalem. He did what was evil in the sight of the Lord his God. [6]Against him came up Nebuchadnezzar king of Babylon, and bound him in fetters to take him to Babylon. [7]Nebuchadnezzar also carried part of the vessels of the house of the Lord to Babylon and put them in his palace in Babylon. [8]Now the rest of the acts of Jehoiakim, and the abominations which he did, and what was found against him, behold, they are written in the Book of the Kings of Israel and Judah; and Jehoiachin his son reigned in his stead.

[9]Jehoiachin was eight years old when he began to reign, and he reigned three months and ten days in Jerusalem. He did what was evil in the sight of the Lord. [10]In the spring of the year King Nebuchadnezzar sent and brought him to Babylon, with the precious vessels of the house of the Lord, and made his brother Zedekiah king over Judah and Jerusalem.

[11]Zedekiah was twenty-one years old when he began to reign, and he reigned eleven years in Jerusalem. [12]He did what was evil in the sight of the Lord his God. He did not humble himself before Jeremiah the prophet, who spoke from the mouth of the Lord. [13]He also rebelled against King Nebuchadnezzar, who had made him swear by God; he stiffened his neck and hardened his heart against turning to the Lord, the God of Israel. [14]All the leading priests and the people likewise were exceedingly unfaithful, following all the abominations of the nations; and they polluted the house of the Lord which he had hallowed in Jerusalem.

[15]The Lord, the God of their fathers, sent persistently to them by his messengers, because he had compassion on

his people and on his dwelling place; [16]but they kept
mocking the messengers of God, despising his words, and
scoffing at his prophets, till the wrath of the Lord rose
against his people, till there was no remedy.

[17]Therefore he brought up against them the king of the
Chaldeans, who slew their young men with the sword in
the house of their sanctuary, and had no compassion on
young man or virgin, old man or aged; he gave them all
into his hand. [18]And all the vessels of the house of God,
great and small, and the treasures of the house of the
Lord, and the treasures of the king and of his princes, all
these he brought to Babylon. [19]And they burned the
house of God, and broke down the wall of Jerusalem, and
burned all its palaces with fire, and destroyed all its
precious vessels. [20] He took into exile in Babylon those
who had escaped from the sword, and they became servants to him and to his sons until the establishment of the
kingdom of Persia, [21]to fulfil the word of the Lord by the
mouth of Jeremiah, until the land had enjoyed its sabbaths. All the days that it lay desolate it kept sabbath, to
fulfil seventy years.

[22]Now in the first year of Cyrus king of Persia, that the
word of the Lord by the mouth of Jeremiah might be
accomplished, the Lord stirred up the spirit of Cyrus king
of Persia so that he made a proclamation throughout all
his kingdom and also put it in writing: [23]"Thus says
Cyrus king of Persia, 'The Lord, the God of heaven, has
given me all the kingdoms of the earth, and he has
charged me to build him a house at Jerusalem, which is in
Judah. Whoever is among you of all his people, may the
Lord his God be with him. Let him go up.' "

The events of this last chapter move as quickly as the
rapid action in an early Charlie Chaplin film; kings are set
up and deposed with bewildering speed and the momentum
builds up until the whole scene suddenly falls to pieces.
Judah's instability in the last years of the kingdom reflects
that of international politics of the time where the star of

Assyria was rapidly waning and that of Babylon was increasingly in the ascendant. The accuracy of the Chronicler's portrayal of the time is confirmed by the archaeological discovery of the *Babylonian Chronicle* which gives a statement of the principal events of the early years of the Babylonian Empire.

Judah was caught in the power politics of the time, particularly through the efforts of Egypt to bolster up the tottering Assyrian Empire. Just as Josiah had fallen victim to these efforts on the part of Egypt so likewise did his son, Jehoahaz, the last king of Judah to be set up by the people themselves. The next king, Jehoiakim, was appointed by the Egyptians and under him the final collapse began. Eleven years after his inauguration, Nebuchadnezzar arrived on the scene and carried him off to Babylon (Dan 1:1-2; but cf. 2 Kings 24:6). He was followed in quick succession by his son, Jehoiachin, and his brother, Zedekiah (see p. 17). Revolt on the part of Zedekiah resulted finally in the Fall of Jerusalem, the destruction of the Temple and the continuation of the Exile in Babylon.

Different theological reasons are given in Kings and in Chronicles for the Exile. In Kings it was seen as necessary because of the accumulated guilt of the people which not even the good deeds of a Josiah could outweigh. In Chronicles, because of the doctrine of individual retribution which implied that no guilt was held over from one generation to the next, the blame for the Exile is laid squarely on the shoulders of Zedekiah and his nobles. They had been offered a chance to repent by the preaching of Jeremiah and other prophets (cf. Jer 37:2) but, says the Chronicler, their stubborn refusal plunged the people headlong into ruin. So the Chronicler's message of individual retribution of each king being rewarded or punished according to his deeds is rigorously adhered to until the end.

Retribution, however, is not the Chronicler's last word. A ray of hope shines through in his statement about the land "keeping Sabbath." This refers to the Israelite law of letting the land lie fallow every seven years so that it could be purified and enriched (cf. Lev 26:34-35). So too the Exile will be a time of purification for the people and will in due time come to an end. The time for this reversal is given as "seventy years" and this is associated with the "word of the Lord by the prophet Jeremiah" which recalls Jer 25:11 (cf. 29:10): "This whole land shall become a ruin and a waste, and these nations shall serve the king of Babylon seventy years." If one counts from the fall of Jerusalem (587) to the conquest of Bablyon by Cyrus (539) the Exile lasted only about fifty years. The Chronicler may have been thinking, however, in terms of the restoration of the Temple in 516. On the other hand, 70 may have been chosen as a round figure or as a link with the Sabbath rest.

In the last section of the book (36:22-23), the return from Exile is anticipated by the promulgation of the Edict of Cyrus the Persian, allowing the captives to return home again (see Ezra 1:2-4). This is a complete reversal of what had happened under the last kings of Judah; the vessels which had been taken from the Temple are to be restored. This would ensure the renewal of Temple worship and so the continuity between the first and second Temple is guaranteed.

Ezra - Nehemiah

AS WAS POINTED OUT in the Introduction (see p. 9), there is no unanimity among scholars about the composition and authorship of the books of Ezra and Nehemiah. Those who continue to hold for the same author as for Chronicles can point to the obvious continuity between the two works, while those who would wish to separate them put forward many proofs of discontinuity. The most recent scholarship would try to do justice to the evidence both of continuity and of discontinuity. One way of doing this is to posit an original edition of the Chronicler's history which would have continued on into the book of Ezra. In this view, the contents of Ezra 1 - 3 and 6:14-18 would be the closest to the thought world of the Chronicler. There is little unanimity among scholars however, as to what could have happened after this initial stage. Some would hold that the Ezra material was next incorporated into the Chronicler's history and, in a later edition, the Nehemiah Memoirs (see p. 177) were added in, disrupting the order of the Ezra material in the process. Others would suggest that the Ezra material was added in at the last stage in the composition of the books and was formed as "memoirs" of Ezra on analogy with the Nehemiah Memoirs. Various other sources available in post-exilic times were also pressed into service: census and other lists (e.g. Ezra 2:1-67; Neh 11:3-36) and documents purporting to come from Persian records (e.g. Ezra 4:8-22; 7:12-26).

Whatever the mix, and however long the process, the

work of the final editor seems to have been a deliberate arrangement of the material at his disposal. His purpose appears to have been to parallel the books of Ezra and Nehemiah with each other and to parallel the work of the reconstruction of the post-exilic community with that of David and Solomon in the construction of the first Temple. Ezra 1 - 6, for instance, which is concerned with rebuilding the Temple can be paralleled with Neh 1 - 7, on the rebuilding of the city walls; both accomplished against opposition. The provision for Ezra's work and return in Ezra 7 is fulfilled in Ezra's reading of the Law (Neh 8). The prayer in Ezra 9 is matched by the prayer in Nehemiah 9. Ezra 10 is an account of the removal of foreign wives by Ezra as is Nehemiah 10 and 13 by Nehemiah. Lists perform the same function in both books by showing the ingathering of the exiles and the land repeopled (e.g. Ezra 2 and Nehemiah 7). The final section in the book of Nehemiah presents a well-ordered and smooth-running Temple with contributions flowing in from the people (12:44-47; 13:12-14). This is a complement to the frequently portrayed picture in Chronicles of what a well-run Temple should look like (e.g. 2 Chron 8:12-16; 31:2-21) Another obvious parallel to Chronicles is that between the foundations of the first Temple and of the second (see p. 156).

The order of the books of Ezra and Nehemiah, therefore, has to be seen as theological rather than as chronological. They can best be divided into the following sections:

I. Return from Exile and Restoration of the Temple (Ezra 1 - 6)

II. Sending of Ezra and Purification of the Temple (Ezra 7 - 10)

III. Sending of Nehemiah and Reconstruction of the City Walls (Neh 1 - 7)

IV. Ceremonies and Reforms of Ezra and Nehemiah (Neh 8 - 13).

I. RETURN FROM EXILE AND RESTORATION OF THE TEMPLE Ezra 1:1—6:22.

THE EDICT OF CYRUS
1:1-4

1 In the first year of Cyrus king of Persia, that the word of the Lord by the mouth of Jeremiah might be accomplished, the Lord stirred up the spirit of Cyrus king of Persia so that he made a proclamation throughout all his kingdom and also put it in writing:

²"Thus says Cyrus king of Persia: The Lord, the God of heaven, has given me all the kingdoms of the earth, and he has charged me to build him a house at Jerusalem, which is in Judah. ³Whoever is among you of all his people, may his God be with him, and let him go up to Jerusalem, which is in Judah, and rebuild the house of the Lord, the God of Israel—he is the God who is in Jerusalem; ⁴and let each survivor, in whatever place he sojourns, be assisted by the men of his place with silver and gold, with goods and with beasts, besides freewill offerings for the house of God which is in Jerusalem."

The book of Ezra opens, as the books of Chronicles closed, with the promulgation of an edict of freedom by the Persian king, Cyrus, which effectively put an end to the period of exile in Babylon. Cyrus had taken the city of Babylon without a single blow in 539 B.C. He was regarded as a liberator by the people of Babylon themselves as well as by the captive peoples who had been confined there. The lenient policy of Cyrus and of the Persian kings who came after him was motivated more by politics than by religious sentiment. The Empire had come into being very quickly and military strength alone would not have been sufficient to hold it together. An altogether new concept in the ancient world was, therefore, tried by the Persians: that of unity in diversity. There was a remarkable tolerance of local custom and in particular of religious customs. A people content around its sanctuary, it was felt, would be a loyal people. But that the motivation was political rather than religious, can be seen from the fact that later Persian kings could destroy temples and suppress religious practices when they felt religion led to revolt.

The first act of Cyrus on taking over the Babylonian Empire, therefore, was to restore the images of the gods of all conquered peoples to their temples. As his own inscription puts it: "... to the cities of Ashur and Susa, Agade, Eshnunna, the cities of Zamban, Meturnu, Der, as far as the region of the land Gutium, the holy cities beyond the Tigris whose sanctuaries had been in ruins over a long period, the gods whose abode is in the midst of them, I returned to their places and housed them in lasting abodes." (From the *Cyrus Cylinder* an inscription on clay dealing with the conquest of Babylon by Cyrus).

There is no mention of Jerusalem in the list of sanctuaries outlined but certainly the edict of Ezra 1:1-4 is very much in keeping with the spirit of the Cylinder even though the Jewish colouring of the text would indicate that it does not come from Cyrus' own hand. The return, for instance, is presented as a new Exodus with the Babylonians, as erstwhile conquerors, forced to pay for the journey like the Egyptians of old (Ezra 1:4; cf. Ex 3:21; 11:2-3; 12:35-36).

The text of the Edict has Cyrus being prompted by God to see to the refounding of the Jerusalem Temple. It is for this reason that Cyrus was regarded as a deliverer sent by God in Second Isaiah (cf. Is 44:24-28; 45:13). The policy of Cyrus was looked on as a direct intervention on the part of God and the beginning of a great new departure in his people's history. Again there would be a possibility of worship in the Temple and the people would know that peculiar joy which they could only experience in Jerusalem (cf. Ps 137 (136)).

GOING UP TO JERUSALEM WITH REJOICING
1:5-2:70

⁵Then rose up the heads of the fathers' houses of Judah and Benjamin, and the priests and the Levites, every one whose spirit God had stirred up to rebuild the house of the Lord which is in Jerusalem; ⁶and all who were about them aided them with vessels of silver, with gold, with goods, with beasts, and with costly wares, besides all that was freely offered. ⁷Cyrus the king also brought out the vessels of the house of the Lord which Nebuchadnezzar had carried away from Jerusalem and placed in the house of his gods. ⁸Cyrus king of Persia brought these out in charge of Mithredath the treasurer, who counted them out to Sheshbazzar the prince of Judah. ⁹And this was the number of them: a thousand basins of gold, a thousand basins of silver, twenty-nine censers, ¹⁰thirty bowls of gold, two thousand four hundred and ten bowls of silver, and a thousand other vessels; ¹¹all the vessels of gold and of silver were five thousand four hundred and sixty-nine. All these did Sheshbazzar bring up, when the exiles were brought up from Babylonia to Jerusalem. 2 Now these were the people of the province who came up out of the captivity of those exiles whom Nebuchadnezzar the king of Babylon had carried captive to Babylonia; they returned to Jerusalem and Judah, each to his own town. ²They came with Zerubbabel, Jeshua, Nehemiah, Seraiah, Reelaiah, Mordecai, Bilshan, Mispar, Bigvai, Rehum, and Baanah . . . . ⁷⁰The priests, the Levites, and some of the people

lived in Jerusalem and its vicinity; and the singers, the gatekeepers, and the temple servants lived in their towns, and all Israel in their towns.

The impression is given that as soon as the decree of Cyrus was promulgated the leaders of the people made one rush for Jerusalem. Laden down with gifts and the vessels which had been stolen from the Temple by the Babylonians, they are presented in liturgical procession wending their way to the city. The reality could hardly be further from the truth as subsequent chapters will make clear. It is more than likely that very few actually availed of the possibility of returning at this early stage. They had settled down in Babylon and did not want to uproot themselves again. One has only to think of the reaction today to a similar request to a group of emigrants to return to an impoverished homeland to realise the reluctance of the exiles in Babylon.

Those who did return were under the leadership of one Sheshbazzar who is given the title of prince and of governor (5:14) but never that of king. The role of Sheshbazzar is confused; memory of his work had grown dim by the time Ezra was written. Actions attributed to him are also attributed to his successor, Zerubbabel (1:11; cf. 2:2). All that can be said for certain about him is that he led back a small contingent of exiles and had something to do with the recommencing of cultic practice in Jerusalem.

The list of returned exiles which follows in chapter two is repeated again in Nehemiah 7 (cf. also 1 Chron 9). It is supposed to be the full complement of all the returnees listed according to their families and towns. There are many theories as to the origin of these lists; the list given here is probably too detailed to be the names of the actual people who returned in 538 B.C. The nearest possibility is that it is the list of those who returned within the following twenty years or so and was, therefore, combined from various registers, or from lists which gave title to land held. The purpose for which the author used the list in Ezra 2, however, is similar to his use of the genealogies at the beginning of Chronicles. They provide the continuity with the past that is needed to give assurance to the present. The covenant community reestablished in Jerusalem did not just spring up from nowhere; it was solidly based on its past ancestors and should therefore live up to what was expected of it.

THE TEMPLE RESTORED
3:1-6:22

This section is one of the most chronologically confused in the books of Ezra and Nehemiah. Most commentaries offer a rewriting of the order of these chapters with a view to getting nearer to the historical sequence. But it has to be borne in mind that the theological rather than the chronological order is what is important for the arranger of the material here (see p. 148). The aim seems to have been to set out firmly the fact of the restoration of the Temple in Jerusalem after the return from Exile and in spite of grave opposition. This rebuilding comes about in three stages:

a) the reestablishment of worship (3:1-13)

b) obstructions put in the way of rebuilding the Temple (4:1-6:13)

c) the actual rebuilding (5:1-2; 6:14-15).

Even though chronology is not the primary aim of the chapters it will help greatly in unravelling their contents if we set out here a table of the historical events as they actually took place. This has been compiled with the aid, in particular, of the books of Haggai and Zechariah, prophets contemporary with the Restoration, and from Persian records.

539 B.C.	Conquest of Babylon by Cyrus
537	Temporary mission of Sheshbazzar
522-486	Reign of Persian king, Darius I
521	Return of exiles under Zerubbabel

520	Prophets Haggai and Zechariah active in Jerusalem
22.9.520	Beginning of work on Temple
December, 520	Foundation stone of Temple laid
518	Inspection by governor, Tattenai, from province "Beyond the River"
13.3.515	Consecration of Temple
486-465	Reign of Xerxes
465-424	Reign of Artaxerxes I
459 (?)	Commissioning of Ezra (see p. 164)
445	Commissioning of Nehemiah
423-404	Reign of Darius II
404-358	Reign of Artaxerxes II
358-338	Reign of Artaxerxes III
336-331	Reign of Darius III and end of Persian Empire

a) The Reestablishment of Worship
3:1-13

3 When the seventh month came, and the sons of Israel were in the towns, the people gathered as one man to Jerusalem. ²Then arose Jeshua the son of Jozadak, with his fellow priests, and Zerubbabel the son of Shealtiel with his kinsmen, and they built the altar of the God of Israel, to offer burnt offerings upon it, as it is written in the law of Moses the man of God. ³They set the altar in its place, for fear was upon them because of the peoples of the lands, and they offered burnt offerings upon it to the Lord, burnt offerings morning and evening . . . .

⁶From the first day of the seventh month they began to offer burnt offerings to the Lord. But the foundation of the temple of the Lord was not yet laid. ⁷So they gave money to the masons and the carpenters, and food, drink, and oil to the Sidonians and the Tyrians to bring cedar trees from Lebanon to the sea, to Joppa, according to the grant which they had from Cyrus king of Persia.

⁸Now in the second year of their coming to the house
of God at Jerusalem, in the second month, Zerubbabel
the son of Shealtiel and Jeshua the son of Jozadak made
a beginning, together with the rest of their brethren,
the priests and the Levites and all who had come to
Jerusalem from the captivity. They appointed the
Levites, from twenty years old and upward, to have the
oversight of the work of the house of the Lord . . . .
¹⁰And when the builders laid the foundation of the
temple of the Lord, the priests in their vestments came
forward with trumpets, and the Levites, the sons of
Asaph, with cymbals, to praise the Lord, according to
the directions of David king of Israel; ¹¹and they sang
responsively, praising and giving thanks to the Lord,
"For he is good,
    for his steadfast love endures for ever toward Israel."
And all the people shouted with a great shout, when they
praised the Lord, because the foundation of the house
of the Lord was laid. ¹²But many of the priests and
Levites and heads of fathers' houses, old men who had
seen the first house, wept with a loud voice when they saw
the foundation of this house being laid, though many
shouted aloud for joy; ¹³so that the people could not
distinguish the sound of the joyful shout from the sound
of the people's weeping, for the people shouted with a
great shout, and the sound was heard afar.

The opening verse of chapter three is almost identical
with Neh 7:73b-8:1 where it forms the conclusion to the
same list which we have just had in 2:1-70. It is used here to
head the notice about the reestablishment of worship. The
year is not given and one would expect that we were now
going to hear about the initial return under Sheshbazzar
(cf. 1:8; 5:16). Instead the later leader, Zerubbabel, and
the priest, Jeshua, are mentioned. It is clear that the earlier
return when only the altar was established (v.3) is confused
with the later setting up of the Temple. The point, however,

is made that at least worship was restored at the return; the taking-up again of the old forms of worship guarantees continuity with the past (3:3-6).

The remainder of the chapter deals with the later period of the reestablishment of the Temple when the foundations were at last laid amid scenes of celebration and rejoicing (3:7-13). Such scenes are reminiscent of many in Chronicles, the refrain of Ps 136(135) reappearing here: "For he is good, for his steadfast love endures forever" (cf. 2 Chron 5:13). The new foundation is deliberately paralleled with that of the first Temple (see p. 148): masons and carpenters are brought in (3:7; cf. 1 Chron 22:2,5); the wood comes from Tyre and Sidon (3:7; cf. 1 Chron 22:4; 2 Chron 2:8) and is paid for in the same way (cf. 2 Chron 2:10). All is in readiness for a new departure which would rival that of the first Temple but those who had actually known of the dimensions of the first Temple and its splendour could not but weep at the poverty of the effort being made (cf. Hag 2:3). Most, however, are glad that at least a beginning has been attempted.

b) *Obstruction of Temple Building*
4:1-6:13

4 Now when the adversaries of Judah and Benjamin heard that the returned exiles were building a temple to the Lord, the God of Israel, [2]they approached Zerubbabel and the heads of fathers' houses and said to them, "Let us build with you; for we worship your God as you do, and we have been sacrificing to him ever since the days of Esarhaddon king of Assyria who brought us here." [3]But Zerubbabel, Jeshua, and the rest of the heads of fathers' houses in Israel said to them, "You have nothing to do with us in building a house to our God; but we alone will build to the Lord, the God of Israel, as King Cyrus the king of Persia has commanded us."

[4]Then the people of the land discouraged the people of Judah, and made them afraid to build, [5]and hired counselors against them to frustrate their purpose, all

the days of Cyrus king of Persia, even until the reign of Darius king of Persia.

⁶And in the reign of Ahasuerus, in the beginning of his reign, they wrote an accusation against the inhabitants of Judah and Jerusalem.

⁷And in the days of Artaxerxes, Bishlam and Mithredath and Tabeel and the rest of their associates wrote to Artaxerxes king of Persia; the letter was written in Aramaic and translated. ⁸Rehum the commander and Shimshai the scribe wrote a letter against Jerusalem to Artaxerxes the king as follows—⁹then wrote Rehum the commander, Shimshai the scribe, and the rest of their associates, the judges, the governors, the officials, the Persians, the men of Erech, the Babylonians, the men of Susa, that is, the Elamites, ¹⁰and the rest of the nations whom the great and noble Osnappar deported and settled in the cities of Samaria and in the rest of the province Beyond the River, and now ¹¹this is a copy of the letter that they sent—"To Artaxerxes the king: Your servants, the men of the province Beyond the River, send greeting. And now ¹²be it known to the king that the Jews who came up from you to us have gone to Jerusalem. They are rebuilding that rebellious and wicked city; they are finishing the walls and repairing the foundations. ¹³Now be it known to the king that, if this city is rebuilt and the walls finished, they will not pay tribute, custom, or toll, and the royal revenue will be impaired. ¹⁴Now because we eat the salt of the palace and it is not fitting for us to witness the king's dishonor, therefore we send and inform the king, ¹⁵in order that search may be made in the book of the records of your fathers. You will find in the book of the records and learn that this city is a rebellious city, hurtful to kings and provinces, and that sedition was stirred up in it from of old. That was why this city was laid waste. ¹⁶We make known to the king that, if this city is rebuilt and its walls finished, you will then have no possession in the province Beyond the River."

¹⁷The king sent an answer: "To Rehum the commander

and Shimshai the scribe and the rest of their associates who live in Samaria and in the rest of the province Beyond the River, greeting. And now [18]the letter which you sent to us has been plainly read before me. [19]And I made a decree, and search has been made, and it has been found that this city from of old has risen against kings, and that rebellion and sedition have been made in it. [20]And mighty kings have been over Jerusalem, who ruled over the whole province Beyond the River, to whom tribute, custom, and toll were paid. [21]Therefore make a decree that these men be made to cease, and that this city be not rebuilt, until a decree is made by me. [22]And take care not to be slack in this matter; why should damage grow to the hurt of the king?"

[23]Then, when the copy of King Artaxerxes' letter was read before Rehum and Shimshai the scribe and their associates, they went in haste to the Jews at Jerusalem and by force and power made them cease. [24]Then the work on the house of God which is in Jerusalem stopped; and it ceased until the second year of the reign of Darius king of Persia.

In these chapters an effort is being made to come to an understanding of the reason why the people were so tardy in doing the very work for which they had returned to the land in the first place: the reconstruction of the Temple. In the book of the prophet Haggai, the blame is laid on the shoulders of the exiles themselves; they were lazy about the rebuilding, insisting on providing their own houses first before touching the Temple (Hag 1:1-10). But here the blame is put, rather, on the enemies of the returned exiles. These are shown to obstruct the work at every possible opportunity. Before continuing with the account of the actual rebuilding, therefore, the obstructions which came in the way of the post-exilic community are listed, whether these actually applied to the rebuilding of the Temple or not. **Obstruction of the community was the same as obstructing the work of the Temple.**

The interpretations range from the reign of Cyrus (4:4-5); through Darius (4:1-3; 5:3-17) into the reign of his successors, Xerxes and Artaxerxes (4:6-23). This latter section obviously has no bearing on the interruption of the work on the Temple - it deals rather with the building of the city walls which was not undertaken until the time of Nehemiah - but it is probably included here because of a desire to bring together the different oppositions to the true community. This latter opposition under Artaxerxes may have been well-known, so what is being said in effect is: the earlier oppositions were every bit as bad as this one you know about.

It is difficult to say exactly who were the actual opponents of the returned exiles. Ezra 4:2 speaks of what were probably the peoples planted by the Assyrians in the Northern Kingdom after the Fall of Samaria in 721 (cf. v.10; 2 Kings 17). Ezra 4:4, however, designates the opponents as "the people of the land," an expression which probably in this case means the people who filled the vacuum in Judah after the deportations to Babylon in 587 and 597 B.C. Ezra 9:1 seems to imply that these were foreigners (cf. 9:11; 10:2). The feeling of opposition is heightened in the following verses (4:6-23) by the piling up of names of important people of the time and of various officials of the Persian administration (cf. 5:3-17). Most of these would have been locals, administering the Province of Samaria of which Judah was only a subsection at this stage; Samaria itself belonged to the fifth Satraphy, "Beyond the River," which comprised that part of the Persian Empire from the Euphrates to the Mediterranean. None of these groups can be identified with the later Samaritans.

There is a definite closing of ranks, therefore, in this section of Ezra against all who were considered as outsiders. The supposition here is that the group of returning exiles were the only true worshippers of Yahweh; they alone, therefore, could rebuild the Temple.

c) Rebuilding the Temple
5:1-6:22

5 Now the prophets, Haggai and Zechariah the son of Iddo, prophesied to the Jews who were in Judah and Jerusalem, in the name of the God of Israel who was over them. ²Then Zerubbabel the son of Shealtiel and Jeshua the son of Jozadak arose and began to rebuild the house of God which is in Jerusalem; and with them were the prophets of God, helping them.

²At the same time Tattenai the governor of the province Beyond the River and Shetharbozenai and their associates came to them and spoke to them thus, "Who gave you a decree to build this house and to finish this structure?" ⁴They also asked them this, "What are the names of the men who are building this building?" ⁵But the eye of their God was upon the elders of the Jews, and they did not stop them till a report should reach Darius and then answer be returned by letter concerning it.

. . . . ⁷they sent him a report, in which was written as follows: "To Darius the king, all peace. ⁸Be it known to the king that we went to the province of Judah, to the house of the great God. It is being built with huge stones, and timber is laid in the walls; this work goes on diligently and prospers in their hands. ⁹Then we asked those elders and spoke to them thus, 'Who gave you a decree to build this house and to finish this structure?' ¹⁰We also asked them their names, for your information, that we might write down the names of the men at their head. ¹¹And this was their reply to us: 'We are the servants of the God of heaven and earth, and we are rebuilding the house that was built many years ago, which a great king of Israel built and finished. . . . ¹⁷Therefore, if it seem good to the king, let search be made in the royal archives there in Babylon, to see whether a decree was issued by Cyrus the king for the rebuilding of this house of God in Jerusalem. And let the king send us his pleasure in this matter."

6 Then Darius the king made a decree, and search was

made in Babylonia, in the house of the archives where the documents were stored. ²And in Ecbatana, the capital which is in the province of Media, a scroll was found on which this was written: "A record. ³In the first year of Cyrus the king, Cyrus the king issued a decree: Concerning the house of God at Jerusalem, let the house be rebuilt, the place where sacrifices are offered and burnt offerings are brought; its height shall be sixty cubits and its breadth sixty cubits, ⁴with three courses of great stones and one course of timber; let the cost be paid from the royal treasury. ⁵And also let the gold and silver vessels of the house of God, which Nebuchadnezzar took out of the temple that is in Jerusalem and brought to Babylon, be restored and brought back to the temple which is in Jerusalem, each to its place; you shall put them in the house of God."

⁶"Now therefore, Tattenai, governor of the province Beyond the River, Shetharbozenai, and your associates the governors who are in the province Beyond the River, keep away; ⁷let the work on this house of God alone; let the governor of the Jews and the elders of the Jews rebuild this house of God on its site. ⁸Moreover I make a decree regarding what you shall do for these elders of the Jews for the rebuilding of this house of God; the cost is to be paid to these men in full and without delay from the royal revenue, the tribute of the province from Beyond the River . . . .

¹³Then, according to the word sent by Darius the king, Tattenai, the governor of the province Beyond the River, Shetharbozenai, and their associates did with all diligence what Darius the king had ordered. ¹⁴And the elders of the Jews built and prospered, through the prophesying of Haggai the prophet and Zechariah the son of Iddo. They finished their building by command of the God of Israel and by decree of Cyrus and Darius and Artaxerxes king of Persia; ¹⁵and this house was finished on the third day of the month of Adar, in the sixth year of the reign of Darius the king . . . .

¹⁹On the fourteenth day of the first month the returned exiles kept the passover. ²⁰For the priests and the Levites had purified themselves together; all of them were clean. So they killed the passover lamb for all the returned exiles, for their fellow priests, and for themselves; ²¹it was eaten by the people of Israel who had returned from exile, and also by every one who had joined them and separated himself from the pollutions of the peoples of the land to worship the Lord.

The account of the opposition under Darius I comes in its proper place historically, that is in the narrative concerning the actual rebuilding of the Temple. Spurred on by the enthusiastic preaching of Haggai and Zechariah, the reconstruction of the Temple is at last undertaken in the second year of Darius. There was much upheaval throughout the Empire at the beginning of this king's reign and the building of the Temple originally may have had political overtones. Certainly Haggai seemed inclined to look on Zerubbabel as the reviver of the Davidic dynasty (Hag 2:23) and it is probable that there were expectations of independence abroad at the time. If there were they did not last long and the book of Ezra preserves no memory of them. In the books of Haggai and Zechariah, the prophets appear to include the reinstitution of the monarchy as well as the reconstruction of the Temple in their restoration program (cf. Hag 2:20-23; Zech 4:6-7); in Ezra-Nehemiah the prophets are concerned with the reconstruction of the Temple alone (see Intro. p. 6). On the completion of the Temple, Zerubbabel disappears and in succeeding years the leadership passes more and more to the high priest.

The inspection by Tattenai, the governor of the province "Beyond the River," would fit naturally into this situation. The origin of the lists in chapter two could also lie here - as a response to his demand for the names of the men engaged in the rebuilding program. The matter is reported to Darius and search is made to see if the rebuilding of the Temple had really been authorised by Cyrus. A document is found which authenticates the matter. This document is quite in keeping with the contents of the edict of Cyrus in 1:1-4 and, because it is in Aramaic, the official language of records at the time, many feel that it is the more original document. Whether authentic or not, it certainly was regarded as such by the author and the outcome is recorded as beneficial to the people of Judah. The Temple is rebuilt and finished in the "sixth year of the reign of Darius" which would have been in the year 515 B.C.

As in the building of the first Temple, a solemn dedicatory service is performed (6:6-18; cf. 2 Chron 7:4-6) and the priests and Levites take up their accustomed positions. But all is on a much smaller scale; sacrifices consist of a mere hundred bulls, two hundred rams, etc., instead of the thousands in Solomon's time. Granted that the figures of the books of Ezra are more realistic than those of Chronicles, yet the contrast does point out the poverty of the new beginning. However, as in the reigns of Hezekiah and Josiah, a new Passover is celebrated and there is great joy among those who had returned and among those "who had joined them and separated themselves from the pollutions of the peoples of the land." These could have been either converts from the North (cf. 2 Chron 30:1) or proselytes from the peoples who had encroached on the land at the time of the Exile (see p. 159). This shows that the returnees were not as totally exclusive as chapter four would imply but could accept as co-worshippers those people who, though they had never been in exile, were prepared to conform to the ideals of purity in worship and life which were being adhered to in Jerusalem. It reechoes the concern of the books of Chronicles to have "all Israel" present at all the major events in their history.

II. THE SENDING OF EZRA AND THE PURIFICATION OF THE TEMPLE
Ezra 7:1—10:44

EZRA IS COMMISSIONED
7:1-26

7 Now after this, in the reign of Artaxerxes king of Persia, Ezra the son of Seraiah, son of Azariah, son of Hilkiah, ²son of Shallum, son of Zadok, son of Ahitub, ³son of Amariah, son of Azariah, son of Meraioth, ⁴son of Zerahiah, son of Uzzi, son of Bukki, ⁵son of Abishua, son of Phinehas, son of Eleazar, son of Aaron the chief priest—⁶this Ezra went up from Babylonia. He was a scribe skilled in the law of Moses which the Lord the God of Israel had given; and the king granted him all that he asked, for the hand of the Lord his God was upon him.

¹¹This is a copy of the letter which King Artaxerxes gave to Ezra the priest, the scribe, learned in matters of the commandments of the Lord and his statutes for Israel: ¹²"Artaxerxes, king of kings, to Ezra the priest, the scribe of the law of the God of heaven. And now ¹³I make a decree that any one of the people of Israel or their priests or Levites in my kingdom, who freely offers to go to Jerusalem, may go with you. ¹⁴For you are sent by the king and his seven counselors to make inquiries

about Judah and Jerusalem according to the law of your God, which is in your hand, [15]and also to convey the silver and gold which the king and his counselors have freely offered to the God of Israel, whose dwelling is in Jerusalem, [16]with all the silver and gold which you shall find in the whole province of Babylonia, and with the freewill offerings of the people and the priests, vowed willingly for the house of their God which is in Jerusalem. [17]With this money, then, you shall with all diligence buy bulls, rams, and lambs, with their cereal offerings and their drink offerings, and you shall offer them upon the altar of the house of your God which is in Jerusalem. [18]Whatever seems good to you and your brethren to do with the rest of the silver and gold, you may do, according to the will of your God. [19]The vessels that have been given you for the service of the house of your God, you shall deliver before the God of Jerusalem. [20]And whatever else is required for the house of your God, which you have occasion to provide, you may provide it out of the king's treasury. . . .

[25]"And you, Ezra, according to the wisdom of your God which is in your hand, appoint magistrates and judges who may judge all the people in the province Beyond the River, all such as know the laws of your God; and those who do not know them, you shall teach. [26]Whoever will not obey the law of your God and the law of the king, let judgment be strictly executed upon him, whether for death or for banishment or for confiscation of his goods or for imprisonment."

"Now after this, in the reign of Artaxerxes. king of Persia,... in the seventh year of Artaxerxes the king..."
—these few words obscure a whole era of history and much ink has flowed in the effort to unravel their implications. There were three Persian kings named Artaxerxes, though for this period only the first two need concern us. The first reigned from 465-424 B.C. and the second from 404-358 B.C. In almost every commentary

on the book of Ezra the reasons for and against Ezra's coming to Jerusalem during one or other of these reigns, are debated. The following chart gives a summary of the positions; there are solid arguments for and against each of them:

1. As the books appear in the Bible, Ezra is sent from the Persian court to carry out a religious reform before Nehemiah comes to see to the physical welfare of the city of Jerusalem. The date of Nehemiah can be fixed by external evidence to 445 B.C.; this would mean that Ezra arrived in 459 B.C., in the seventh year of Artaxerxes I (Ezra 7:8).

2. Since the physical construction work of Nehemiah was more likely to have preceded the reform of Ezra, many scholars find evidence in the text to believe that Ezra came in the seventh year of Artaxerxes the *second* rather than the first; this would mean that he did not arrive until 398 B.C.

3. This would appear to be rather late so many look elsewhere for a solution. A slight textual correction would give the *thirty-seventh* year of the king rather than the seventh. Now Artaxerxes the first did have quite a long reign and the thirty-seventh year would be in 428 B.C. which does fit in with some of the data of Ezra though not with all.

Whatever the solution historically, there is no doubt that it is not where the main interest of the author lies. For him the theological meaning is, as always, uppermost (see p. 148). In his account of the restoration of the people after the Exile the next most important event after the rebuilding of the Temple was the coming of Ezra, the man who was to structure the community on the solid foundation of the Law of their God. The "Now after this" with which the chapter begins is yet once again not a chronological notice; it is more a statement of priority. The intention is to proceed to the next most important event in the reconstitution of the people of Judah as the people of God.

The pedigree and function of Ezra is outlined in detail; he is made to belong to the priestly line as a descendant of Aaron. He is named as the son of Seraiah, the last officiating priest of pre-exilic times (cf. 2 Kgs 25:18-21). As was pointed out in the section of Chronicles dealing with genealogies, "son of" implies the fact of his being the legitimate priestly successor rather than meaning biological sonship. Ezra is also described as a scribe. This may mean that he was an official of the Persian court, even, it has been suggested, a secretary for Jewish affairs. But, in the text, the official idea of a Persian scribe is confused with that of a later Jewish scribe - one who would read and expound the Law of God (7:6; cf. Neh 8:8). These scribes would be increasingly seen as successors of the prophets. Ezra is presented as finding great favour with the Persian king and being given great power, even the power to impose the death penalty (7:26).

His commission is set out in the form of a letter from the king. The language of this document is again Aramaic as in the official documents mentioned in earlier chapters. This letter probably has a historical core which gave the religion of Judah an official status within the Persian Empire as a permitted religion whose law was recognised by the state. But the present form of the letter has been expanded. As it stands it deals with three important aspects of Ezra's mission:

a) permission for any Jewish settlers in Babylon to return to Jerusalem with Ezra;

b) Ezra to make enquiries concerning the state of affairs in Judah and Jerusalem and to present the Law of Moses as the law of the state;

c) financial contributions to the Temple.

EZRA SETS OUT
7:27-8:36

²⁷Blessed be the Lord, the God of our fathers, who put such a thing as this into the heart of the king, to beautify the house of the Lord which is in Jerusalem, ²⁸and who extended to me his steadfast love before the king and his counselors, and before all the king's mighty officers. I took courage, for the hand of the Lord my God was upon me, and I gathered leading men from Israel to go up with me.

8 These are the heads of their fathers' houses, and this is the genealogy of those who went up with me from Babylonia, in the reign of Artaxerxes the king: ²Of the sons of Phinehas, Gershom. Of the sons of Ithamar, Daniel. Of the sons of David, Hattush....

²¹Then I proclaimed a fast there, at the river Ahava, that we might humble ourselves before our God, to seek from him a straight way for ourselves, our children, and all our goods. ²²For I was ashamed to ask the king for a band of soldiers and horsemen to protect us against the enemy on our way; since we had told the king, "The hand of our God is for good upon all that seek him, and the power of his wrath is against all that forsake him." ²³So we fasted and besought our God for this, and he listened to our entreaty.

²⁴Then I set apart twelve of the leading priests: Sherebiah, Hashabiah, and ten of their kinsmen with them. ²⁵And I weighed out to them the silver and the gold and the vessels, the offering for the house of our God which the king and his counselors and his lords and all Israel there present had offered ....

³¹Then we departed from the river Ahava on the twelfth day of the first month, to go to Jerusalem; the hand of our God was upon us, and he delivered us from the hand of the enemy and from ambushes by the way. ³²We came to Jerusalem, and there we remained three days. ³³On the fourth day, within the house of our God,

the silver and the gold and the vessels were weighed into the hands of Meremoth the priest, son of Uriah, and with him was Eleazar the son of Phinehas, and with them were the Levites, Jozabad the son of Jeshua and Noadiah the son of Binnui. 34The whole was counted and weighed, and the weight of everything was recorded.

35At that time those who had come from captivity, the returned exiles, offered burnt offerings to the God of Israel, twelve bulls for all Israel, ninety-six rams, seventy-seven lambs, and as a sin offering twelve he-goats; all this was a burnt offering to the Lord. 36They also delivered the king's commissions to the king's satraps and to the governors of the province Beyond the River; and they aided the people and the house of God.

Chapter seven ends with a prayer of thanksgiving to God for the action that the King of Persia had taken in favour of the people of Judah. The passage is in the first person and starts off the section which is generally called the "Memoirs of Ezra." Some would see these as going back to Ezra himself but there is an increasing suspicion among scholars that they are rather a composition of the Chronicler put in the form of memoirs to act as a balance to the Memoirs of Nehemiah (Neh 1:1-7:5; 12:31-13:31). The purpose in this would be to point up the complementarity of Ezra and Nehemiah as the two great leaders who built up the post-exilic community (see Intro. p. 9 and p. 148).

The courage Ezra felt in undertaking the work is mentioned (7:28); he and his followers certainly needed it for the trip to Jerusalem as the way was long and arduous. But, in true Chronicler fashion, devout prayer to God ensures their success (8:21-23;31). This is one of the few passages in Ezra-Nehemiah where the Chronicler's theory of retribution is also evident: "The hand of our God is for good upon all that seek him, and the power of his wrath is against all that forsake him." Their departure is again seen as a new Exodus.

Another list begins chapter eight, said to be of the exiles

who returned with Ezra. It is a different list from that in Ezra 2 and Nehemiah 7 and probably comes from an independent source. The number twelve is given prominence in the chapter, probably due to the insistence of the author that all twelve tribes are important for the full complement of the people of Israel. At this new departure, the whole people must again be seen to be present.

The valuables the returnees take with them are entrusted to the priests which they are to hand over on arrival in Jerusalem. As usual on the successful completion of a mission sacrifices are offered when they arrive there. The king's commissions are duly handed over to the relevant Persian authorities and the stage is set for the commencement of Ezra's work.

EZRA'S REFORM MEASURES AND PRAYER
9:1-15

9 After these things had been done, the officials approached me and said, "The people of Israel and the priests and the Levites have not separated themselves from the peoples of the lands with their abominations, from the Canaanites, the Hittites, the Perizzites, the Jebusites, the Ammonites, the Moabites, the Egyptians, and the Amorites. ²For they have taken some of their daughters to be wives for themselves and for their sons; so that the holy race has mixed itself with the peoples of the lands. And in this faithlessness the hand of the officials and chief men has been foremost." ³When I heard this, I rent my garments and my mantle, and pulled hair from my head and beard, and sat appalled.

⁴Then all who trembled at the words of the God of Israel, because of the faithlessness of the returned exiles, gathered round me while I sat appalled until the evening sacrifice. ⁵And at the evening sacrifice I rose from my fasting, with my garments and my mantle rent, and fell upon my knees and spread out my hands to the Lord my

God, ⁶saying:

"O my God, I am ashamed and blush to lift my face to thee, my God, for our iniquities have risen higher than our heads, and our guilt has mounted up to the heavens. ⁷From the days of our fathers to this day we have been in great guilt; and for our iniquities we, our kings, and our priests have been given into the hand of the kings of the lands, to the sword, to captivity, to plundering, and to utter shame, as at this day. ⁸But now for a brief moment favor has been shown by the Lord our God, to leave us a remnant, and to give us a secure hold within his holy place, that our God may brighten our eyes and grant us a little reviving in our bondage. ⁹For we are bondmen; yet our God has not forsaken us in our bondage, but has extended to us his steadfast love before the kings of Persia, to grant us some reviving to set up the house of our God, to repair its ruins, and to give us protection in Judea and Jerusalem.

¹⁰"And now, O our God, what shall we say after this? For we have forsaken thy commandments, ¹¹which thou didst command by thy servants the prophets, saying, 'The land which you are entering, to take possession of it, is a land unclean with the pollutions of the peoples of the lands, with their abominations which have filled it from end to end with their uncleanness. ¹²Therefore give not your daughters to their sons, neither take their daughters for your sons, and never seek their peace or prosperity, that you may be strong, and eat the good of the land and leave it for an inheritance to your children for ever.' ¹³And after all that has come upon us for our evil deeds and for our great guilt, seeing that thou, our God, hast punished us less than our iniquities deserved and hast given us such a remnant as this, ¹⁴shall we break thy commandments again and intermarry with the peoples who practice these abominations? Wouldst thou not be angry with us till thou wouldst consume us, so that there should be no remnant, nor any to escape? ¹⁵O Lord the God of Israel, thou art just,

> for we are left a remnant that has escaped, as at this day.
> Behold, we are before thee in our guilt, for none can
> stand before thee because of this."

The notice at the beginning of chapter nine: "After
these things had been done," hides the interval of time
which must have elapsed between Ezra's arrival and the
reform concerning mixed marriages which he undertook
(cf. 10:9). Again the theological priority takes precedence
over the historical. This time the Chronicler seems concerned to demonstrate the need for a holy community
gathered around the reconstructed holy Temple; he,
therefore, singles out that aspect of Ezra's reform which
was the most important for him and gives it priority.

Prohibition against mixed marriages was nothing new in
Israelite society but, originally, this would have been a
prohibition against marrying outside the tribe in case the
wealth of the tribe would be diminished. In the early
monarchy, marriage patterns depended upon the larger
social, political and economic interaction and so there was
the example of Solomon marrying a Pharaoh's daughter as
well as women from other neighbouring countries. But
the religious implication of such intermarriage was quickly
felt. The books of Kings are loud in their condemnation of
the religious apostasy into which foreign marriage alliances
led Israelite kings and nobles (e.g. 1 Kings 11:1-8). The
small beleagured post-exilic community (see Intro. p. 2, 3),
valiantly striving to keep its identity, was in a particularly
vulnerable position. If the people were to continue marrying
those of alien faith and taking on their beliefs, there would
very soon be no distinctive Jewish group left in Jerusalem
at all.

Ezra's marriage reforms, therefore, have to be seen as a
purification of the people according to a priestly ideal of
separation from all that was unclean for the purpose of
preserving the faith intact. No matter how narrow such an
attitude may appear in the present day, it has to be said
that he was doing what he felt to be absolutely necessary

to ensure the survival of the community - even if he was unpopular in some quarters as a result. That the books of Ezra and Nehemiah do not reflect every current of opinion on the question in the Judah of the time, however, can be seen from the more positive attitude to foreigners in other post-exilic literature.

The prayer which follows the account of reform measures spells out the guilt of the people. There is a modification of the Chronicler's doctrine of retribution here: "seeing that thou, our God, hast punished us *less* than our iniquities deserved..." (9:13; see Intro. p. 8). This is leaning towards the later rabbinic playing off of the justice of God against his mercy. The people should have been wiped out because of their guilt and yet there is still a remnant of them remaining before God. Ezra wants to ensure that they will continue to be such a remnant.

REPENTANCE
10:1-44

10 While Ezra prayed and made confession, weeping and casting himself down before the house of God, a very great assembly of men, women, and children, gathered to him out of Israel; for the people wept bitterly. ²And Shecaniah the son of Jehiel, of the sons of Elam, addressed Ezra: "We have broken faith with our God and have married foreign women from the peoples of the land, but even now there is hope for Israel in spite of this. ³Therefore let us make a covenant with our God to put away all these wives and their children, according to the counsel of my lord and of those who tremble at the commandment of our God; and let it be done according to the law. ⁴Arise, for it is your task, and we are with you; be strong and do it." ⁵Then Ezra arose and made the leading priests and Levites and all Israel take oath that they would do as had been said. So they took the oath.

⁶Then Ezra withdrew from before the house of God,

and went to the chamber of Jehohanan the son of
Eliashib, where he spent the night, neither eating bread
nor drinking water; for he was mourning over the
faithlessness of the exiles. [7]And a proclamation was made
throughout Judah and Jerusalem to all the returned
exiles that they should assemble at Jerusalem, [8]and that if
any one did not come within three days, by order of the
officials and the elders all his property should be for-
feited, and he himself banned from the congregation
of the exiles.

[9]Then all the men of Judah and Benjamin assembled
at Jerusalem within the three days; it was the ninth
month, on the twentieth day of the month. And all the
people sat in the open square before the house of God,
trembling because of this matter and because of the
heavy rain. [10]And Ezra the priest stood up and said to
them, "You have trespassed and married foreign women,
and so increased the guilt of Israel. [11]Now then make
confession to the Lord the God of your fathers, and do
his will; separate yourselves from the peoples of the
land and from the foreign wives." [12]Then all the assembly
answered with a loud voice, "It is so; we must do as you
have said. [13]But the people are many, and it is a time of
heavy rain; we cannot stand in the open. Nor is this a
work for one day or for two; for we have greatly trans-
gressed in this matter. [14]Let our officials stand for the
whole assembly; let all in our cities who have taken
foreign wives come at appointed times, and with them
the elders and judges of every city, till the fierce wrath of
our God over this matter be averted from us." [15]Only
Jonathan the son of Asahel and Jahzeiah the son of
Tikvah opposed this, and Meshullam and Shabbethai
the Levite supported them.

[16]Then the returned exiles did so. Ezra the priest
selected men, heads of fathers' houses, according to their
fathers' houses, each of them designated by name. On the
first day of the tenth month they sat down to examine
the matter; [17]and by the first day of the first month they

had come to the end of all the men who had married foreign women.

Ezra's prayer and persuasion produced the desired result. At first a select group turned to Ezra's way of thinking and they then enforced their opinion on the whole people. A great assembly was convened at which Ezra called for public confession of sin and repentance. The people were dismayed at the gravity of the affair and by the heavy rain (and there is no rain anywhere as cold and as miserable as the winter rain in Jerusalem). Ezra must have had some humanity in him since he granted the people's request for a respite and the work of weeding out those guilty of mixed marriages was left to officials. A list of those who had offended is appended to the chapter (10:18-44). It reads like a *Who's Who* of the times since most of the leading names are there; probably the list only refers to the leading families in any case. Nothing is said about what happened to the unfortunate women and children who were thus separated. Such humanitarian considerations were not even considered. Presumably they went back to their homes and were cared for by their own families.

This section of the book of Ezra would seem to take up once again the concern of the Chronicler for "all Israel" (see Intro. p. 7). The assembly of the people is said to be gathered "out of Israel" (10:1) and the leading priests and Levites and "all Israel' take oath to do as Ezra said (10:5). The foreigners mentioned in the matter of mixed marriages include no mention of Northerners under any name. This would suggest a continuity with the Chronicler's way of looking at things in Chronicles but there is definite development too, as was noted in the area of the theory of retribution (see Intro. p. 7 and p. 173). There is complete novelty in the treatment of the question of mixed marriages. It was so little a burning issue in Chronicles that Solomon is not even chastised, as he was in Kings, for his many foreign wives and their ability to lead him into apostasy.

The divergence which can be traced between the two works does not detract from a central preoccupation which runs like a thread throughout. That is the fact of the post-exilic community gathered around its Temple in the secure possession of faith in its God who alone can save his people from external enemies and internal divisions. In the different episodes of the history, whatever furthered this ideal was to be highlighted; whatever detracted from it was to be ignored or condemned.

III. THE SENDING OF NEHEMIAH AND THE RECONSTRUCTION OF THE CITY WALLS

Neh 1:1 - 7:73

THE BOOK OF NEHEMIAH opens with an extract from what has been called the *Memoirs of Nehemiah* (Neh 1:1-7:5; cf. 2:31-13:31). This is one of the most likely sources to be taken over en bloc and incorporated into the work as a whole (see Intro. p. 9 and p. 147). The Memoirs are written in a very different style from the remainder of Chronicles-Ezra-Nehemiah, with what seems to be eye-witness clarity and directness. They give a clear portrait of Nehemiah as a man with great leadership qualities, one who was not lacking in firmness and courage but who could also use diplomacy and humanity especially towards the poor (cf. Neh 5:1-19). He was a sensible, practical politician but one who was also deeply religious. He showed his religious fervour, however, in doing the necessary practical matters which would preserve the faith of his people intact into the next generation. It is for this reason that an account of his exploits comes after those of Ezra: rebuilding the Temple and promulgating the Law was all very fine, but if there was no practical organisation and no walls around the city, how long would it all last?

Though most scholars down the years have regarded

the Nehemiah Memoirs as coming from the hand of Nehemiah himself, some recent studies would tend to call the Nehemiah material a *Memorial* rather than "Memoirs" and, therefore, written about Nehemiah rather than by him. The Memoirs certainly have many features in common with other ancient biographical inscriptions which were written to remind men and gods of work done and deeds of piety performed. Statements such as: "Remember for my good, O my God, all that I have done for this people" (5:19) are typical of such inscriptions. They are frequent in Nehemiah (cf. 6:9; 13:14,22,31).

THE PLIGHT OF JERUSALEM
1:1-11

1 The words of Nehemiah the son of Hacaliah.

Now it happened in the month of Chislev, in the twentieth year, as I was in Susa the capital, ²that Hanani, one of my brethren, came with certain men out of Judah; and I asked them concerning the Jews that survived, who had escaped exile, and concerning Jerusalem. ³And they said to me, "The survivors there in the province who escaped exile are in great trouble and shame; the wall of Jerusalem is broken down, and its gates are destroyed by fire."

⁴When I heard these words I sat down and wept, and mourned for days; and I continued fasting and praying before the God of heaven. ⁵And I said, "O Lord God of heaven, the great and terrible God who keeps covenant and steadfast love with those who love him and keep his commandments; ⁶let thy ear be attentive, and thy eyes open, to hear the prayer of thy servant which I now pray before thee day and night for the people of Israel thy servants, confessing the sins of the people of Israel, which we have sinned against thee. Yea, I and my father's house have sinned. ⁷We have acted very corruptly against thee, and have not kept the commandments, the statutes,

and the ordinances which thou didst command thy servant Moses. [8]Remember the word which thou didst command thy servant Moses, saying, 'If you are unfaithful, I will scatter you among the peoples; [9]but if you return to me and keep my commandments and do them, though your dispersed be under the farthest skies, I will gather them thence and bring them to the place which I have chosen, to make my name dwell there.' [10]They are thy servants and thy people, whom thou hast redeemed by thy great power and by thy strong hand. [11]O Lord, let thy ear be attentive to the prayer of thy servant, and to the prayer of thy servants who delight to fear thy name; and give success to thy servant today, and grant him mercy in the sight of this man."

Now I was cupbearer to the king.

The practice of seeking help from a relative who has made it in a new country did not begin today nor yesterday and so there is nothing unusual in a delegation from Jerusalem making its way to the highest ranks of the Persian Empire where one of their own had reached the top. It is difficult to say whether the picture of woes which they presented referred to the condition the city had been in since the return from Exile or had resulted from a recent attack. It is more than possible that attempts at rebuilding the walls would have been undertaken before this and so in question here would be a recent attack on the city. Some would suggest that this was a raid by Bedouin tribes to the south. The time is the twentieth year of King Artaxerxes I (v.1). The urgency of the mission and the distressed response of Nehemiah would lend credence to the suggestion that what had happened was something recent.

His reaction takes the form of prayer and fasting which lasted several days. The general tenor of the prayer is given (v.5-11) in what is probably an insertion of the Chronicler. It is full of phrases from the book of Deuteronomy. On the other hand, saying prayers of set formula would be quite a possibility for someone like Nehemiah whose gifts were more practical than contemplative and creative. The prayer emphasises the faithfulness of God and begs him to listen to his people's need in this crisis. Nehemiah acknowledges that the people have sinned and deserve punishment. But repentance can bring them back to God, a theme which is familiar from Chronicles, though at the same time there is an allusion to the Exodus which, as has been demonstrated, was not a feature of Chronicles. The general background of the prayer is linked to the present situation by asking for God's grace on Nehemiah as he goes into the presence of the king.

NEHEMIAH IN THE PRESENCE OF THE KING
2:1-8

2 In the month of Nisan, in the twentieth year of King Artaxerxes, when wine was before him, I took up the wine and gave it to the king. Now I had not been sad in his presence. ²And the king said to me, "Why is your face sad, seeing you are not sick? This is nothing else but sadness of the heart." Then I was very much afraid. ³I said to the king, "Let the king live for ever! Why should not my face be sad, when the city, the place of my fathers' sepulchres, lies waste, and its gates have been destroyed by fire?" ⁴Then the king said to me, "For what do you make request?" So I prayed to the God of heaven. ⁵And I said to the king, "If it pleases the king, and if your servant has found favor in your sight, that you send me to Judah, to the city of my fathers' sepulchres, that I may rebuild it." ⁶And the king said to me (the queen sitting beside him), "How long will you be gone, and when will you return?" So it pleased the king to send me; and I set him a time. ⁷And I said to the king, "If it pleases the king, let letters be given me to the governors of the province Beyond the River, that they may let me pass through until I come to Judah; ⁸and a letter to Asaph, the keeper of the king's forest, that he may give me timber

to make beams for the gates of the fortress of the temple, and for the wall of the city, and for the house which I shall occupy." And the king granted me what I asked, for the good hand of my God was upon me.

Nehemiah's post at the Persian court was that of cup-bearer. This post was not merely that of waiter but implied a position of influence, since it assured regular access to the presence of the king and of the queen (v.6). That the king in question was Artaxerxes the first rather than the second has been proved from contemporary documents. There is quite a gap between Nehemiah's hearing of the plight of Jerusalem and his acquainting the king about the matter. This is not done directly but by the king himself becoming aware of Nehemiah's depression. The delay and alarm could tally with the state of affairs described in Ezra 4:7-23 where an attempt at rebuilding the walls had been stopped by Artaxerxes, probably earlier in his career.

The general condition of the Empire in the time of Artaxerxes the first probably had a lot to do with both the prohibition and the eventual success of Nehemiah in gaining permission for the rebuilding. An earlier revolt in Egypt had finally been crushed only to be followed by a revolt in Syria by one of the king's own chief governors (or *satraps* as they were called). This had only been put down in 448 B.C. Artaxerxes had trouble on the Western front also where the Greeks, flushed by their earlier victories over the Persian fleet (480-479 B.C.), continued to challenge Persian domination. While such revolts were in progress, the Persians would not have tolerated strong fortified cities ruled by men of unknown loyalties, but by 445 B.C. the fortification of Jerusalem and the fact that it would be ruled by one of the king's close collaborators was a very different matter. The city could become an outpost in case of further revolt from neighbouring provinces.

That these political motivations do not appear in the text is quite understandable since the Memoirs would want the permission to rebuild to appear as a personal favour to

Nehemiah from the king. His mandate included the provision of the necessary supplies for the journey and for the rebuilding operations. That these would extend to more than the walls is hinted at here (v.8) as in Sirach where it is said of Nehemiah: "The memory of Nehemiah also is lasting; he raised for us the walls that had fallen, and set up the gates and bars and rebuilt the ruined houses" (Sir 49:13).

NEHEMIAH SETS OUT
2:9-20

⁹Then I came to the governors of the province Beyond the River, and gave them the king's letters. Now the king had sent with me officers of the army and horsemen. ¹⁰But when Sanballat the Horonite and Tobiah the servant, the Ammonite, heard this, it displeased them greatly that some one had come to seek the welfare of the children of Israel.

¹¹So I came to Jerusalem and was there three days. ¹²Then I arose in the night, I and a few men with me; and I told no one what my God had put into my heart to do for Jerusalem. There was no beast with me but the beast on which I rode. ¹³I went out by night by the Valley Gate to the Jackal's Well and to the Dung Gate, and I inspected the walls of Jerusalem which were broken down and its gates which had been destroyed by fire. ¹⁴Then I went on to the Fountain Gate and to the King's Pool; but there was no place for the beast that was under me to pass. ¹⁵Then I went up in the night by the valley and inspected the wall; and I turned back and entered by the Valley Gate, and so returned. ¹⁶And the officials did not know where I had gone or what I was doing; and I had not yet told the Jews, the priests, the nobles, the officials, and the rest that were to do the work.

¹⁷Then I said to them, "You see the trouble we are in, how Jerusalem lies in ruins with its gates burned. Come,

let us build the wall of Jerusalem, that we may no longer suffer disgrace." [18]And I told them of the hand of my God which had been upon me for good, and also of the words which the king had spoken to me. And they said, "Let us rise up and build." So they strengthened their hands for the good work. [19]But when Sanballat the Horonite and Tobiah the servant, the Ammonite, and Geshem the Arab heard of it, they derided us and despised us and said, "What is this thing that you are doing? Are you rebelling against the king?" [20]Then I replied to them, "The God of heaven will make us prosper, and we his servants will arise and build; but you have no portion or right or memorial in Jerusalem."

The checks and balances within the Persian Empire can be inferred from Nehemiah's having to present his credentials to the governors of the areas en route to Jerusalem. Only two of these nearest to Judah are mentioned by name. These two would reappear as Nehemiah's opponents at every stage of the rebuilding of the walls. Their opposition was more political than religious but Nehemiah would object to them chiefly on religious grounds. Interestingly enough, these two must also have been worshippers of Yahweh: from contemporary documents it is clear that Tobiah (the ending "-iah" makes his a Yahweh name) belonged to an influential Judean family. But he is called an Ammonite in the passage here. This may have been because he was the governor of Ammon but it could also imply that he worshipped foreign gods as well as Yahweh (cf. Deut 23:3-5). Likewise with Sanballat. He had given his two sons Yahweh names: Delaiah and Shelemiah, but he is called a Horonite himself. This could merely mean that he was a native of Bethhoran to the north-west of Jerusalem but perhaps it meant that he was also a worshipper of false gods, in particular of the Canaanite god, Horon.

In the absence of strong leadership in Jerusalem Sanballat, as governor of Samaria, had exercised a measure of control there (4:1-9), while Tobiah had intermarried with leading families in Judah who would provide their own opposition to Nehemiah (5:1-13; 6:18-19). The other opponent mentioned in the chapter, Geshem the Arab (2:19), was strictly an outsider. He was the father of Kain, king of Keder, who had an united Arab league going in his day which controlled areas around the Dead Sea and as far as Egypt. Together these opponents, therefore, were a force to be reckoned with by Nehemiah.

On coming to Jerusalem Nehemiah wasted no time; he used his powers of organisation and diplomacy to the full. He first of all made a personal tour of inspection to assess at first hand what was needed by way of reconstruction and only then acquainted the leaders of the people of the reason for his mission, justifying it on religious grounds (2:18). His hearers were prepared for immediate action.

REBUILDING THE WALLS AMID OPPOSITION
3:1-4:23

3 Then Eliashib the high priest rose up with his brethren the priests and they built the Sheep Gate. They consecrated it and set its doors; they consecrated it as far as the Tower of the Hundred, as far as the Tower of Hananel. ²And next to him the men of Jericho built. And next to them Zaccur the son of Imri built.

³And the sons of Hassenaah built the Fish Gate; they laid its beams and set its doors, its bolts, and its bars. ⁴And next to them Meremoth the son of Uriah, son of Hakkoz repaired. And next to them Meshullam the son of Berechiah, son of Meshezabel repaired. And next to them Zadok the son of Baana repaired. ⁵And next to them the Tekoites repaired; but their nobles did not put their necks to the work of their Lord....

4 ⁶So we built the wall; and all the wall was joined together to half its height. For the people had a mind to work.

7But when Sanballat and Tobiah and the Arabs and the Ammonites and the Ashdodites heard that the repairing of the walls of Jerusalem was going forward and that the breaches were beginning to be closed, they were very angry; 8and they all plotted together to come and fight against Jerusalem and to cause confusion in it. 9And we prayed to our God, and set a guard as a protection against them day and night.

10But Judah said, "The strength of the burden-bearers is failing, and there is much rubbish; we are not able to work on the wall." 11And our enemies said, "They will not know or see till we come into the midst of them and kill them and stop the work." 12When the Jews who lived by them came they said to us ten times, "From all the places where they live they will come up against us." 13So in the lowest parts of the space behind the wall, in open places, I stationed the people according to their families, with their swords, their spears, and their bows. 14And I looked, and arose, and said to the nobles and to the officials and to the rest of the people, "Do not be afraid of them. Remember the Lord, who is great and terrible, and fight for your brethren, your sons, your daughters, your wives, and your homes."

15When our enemies heard that it was known to us and that God had frustrated their plan, we all returned to the wall, each to his work. 16From that day on, half of my servants worked on construction, and half held the spears, shields, bows, and coats of mail; and the leaders stood behind all the house of Judah, 17who were building on the wall. Those who carried burdens were laden in such a way that each with one hand labored on the work and with the other held his weapon. 18And each of the builders had his sword girded at his side while he built. The man who sounded the trumpet was beside me. 19And I said to the nobles and to the officials and to the rest of the people, "The work is great and widely spread, and we are separated on the wall, far from one another. 20In the place where your hear the sound of the trumpet, rally to us there. Our God will fight for us."

[21]So we labored at the work, and half of them held the spears from the break of dawn till the stars came out. [22]I also said to the people at that time, "Let every man and his servant pass the night within Jerusalem, that they may be a guard for us by night and may labor by day." [23]So neither I nor my brethren nor my servants nor the men of the guard who followed me, none of us took off our clothes; each kept his weapon in his hand.

A list of those who took part in the rebuilding is given in chapter three. This list interrupts the Memoirs of Nehemiah and, given the prominence of the high priest in it, was probably a list originating from the Temple archives. It has proved a valuable document for understanding the topography of Jerusalem in Persian times. It points up how well planned the undertaking must have been and hides the amount of negotiation and diplomacy used to get such widespread participation. Not all sectors of the population of Judah were willing to lend a hand, however, the nobles in particular being recalcitrant (3:5).

The opposition to Nehemiah's activity intensified as the work got underway. A proverb which was thrown at the builders is quoted: "If a fox goes up on it he will break down their stone wall" (4:3). Parts of Nehemiah's wall have been uncovered in excavations in Jerusalem. What strikes one with amazement on viewing it is the sturdiness of its basic structure given that it was built with such haste and under such difficult circumstances.

Nehemiah's response to his enemies' interference is two-pronged: prayer on the one hand but, on the other, vigorous measures of self-protection. This betrays a different attitude from those passages in Chronicles where the advice seems to be to leave everything to prayer since God will intervene to save the situation (cf. 2 Chron 13). The attitude here is more in keeping with the robust spirituality of Nehemiah as he exhorts his people to "fight for your brethren, your sons, your daughters, your wives and your homes." It is on passages like this in the Bible that the action of pioneers has often been justified. But self-defence has to be distinguished from aggression and the taking over of other people's homes and territory.

SOCIAL REFORM
5:1-13

5 Now there arose a great outcry of the people and of their wives against their Jewish brethren. [2]For there were those who said, "With our sons and our daughters, we are many; let us get grain, that we may eat and keep alive." [3]There were also those who said, "We are mortgaging our fields, our vineyards, and our houses to get grain because of the famine." [4]And there were those who said, "We have borrowed money for the king's tax upon our fields and our vineyards. [5]Now our flesh is as the flesh of our brethren, our children are as their children; yet we are forcing our sons and our daughters to be slaves, and some of our daughters have already been enslaved; but it is not in our power to help it, for other men have our fields and our vineyards."

[6]I was very angry when I heard their outcry and these words. [7]I took counsel with myself, and I brought charges against the nobles and the officials. I said to them, "You are exacting interest, each from his brother." And I held a great assembly against them, [8]and said to them, "We, as far as we are able, have bought back our Jewish brethren who have been sold to the nations; but you even sell your brethren that they may be sold to us!" They were silent, and could not find a word to say. [9]So I said, "The thing that you are doing is not good. Ought you not to walk in the fear of our God to prevent the taunts of the nations our enemies? [10]Moreover I and my brethren and my servants are lending them money and grain. Let us leave off this interest. [11]Return to them

this very day their fields, their vineyards, their olive orchards, and their houses, and the hundredth of money, grain, wine, and oil which you have been exacting of them." [12]Then they said, "We will restore these and require nothing from them. We will do as you say." And I called the priests, and took an oath of them to do as they had promised. [13]I also shook out my lap and said, "So may God shake out every man from his house and from his labor who does not perform this promise. So may he be shaken out and emptied." And all the assembly said "Amen" and praised the Lord. And the people did as they had promised.

Nehemiah was not content merely to provide external security; his next action, prompted by obvious need, was to secure social reform. The Jerusalem of the time was the scene of what often happens in a time of need: those who were rich already get richer on the misery of others. It is interesting to note that it was the women of the society who first cried out against the injustices and against the break-up of family life which they caused. Nehemiah's efforts to rebuild the community (which had broken down as much as the walls) was based solidly on Israelite law which emphasised the necessity for love towards the other members of God's people. The laws concerning the granting of release from debts can be found in Leviticus (25:8-11) and concern for the poor in Deuteronomy (e.g. Deut 15:1-11).

Nehemiah's anger was directed against the nobles and officials since it was they who were beggaring their neighbours by exacting interest, which would not be repaid, on the purchase of necessities. When a warning did not succeed in winning them over, he held a great assembly and won popular support; the nobles were thereby forced to comply. Nehemiah's action of "shaking out his lap" (much as we might turn our pockets inside out) was a symbolic action which implied that they themselves would be left without anything if they did not fulfill their oath. The assembly responds with a fervent "Amen" to Nehemiah's tirade.

"Amen," meaning "so be it," was a form of solemn congregational assent on such occasions and not only in the Liturgy.

NEHEMIAH SETS AN EXAMPLE
5:14-19

[14]Moreover from the time that I was appointed to be their governor in the land of Judah, from the twentieth year to the thirty-second year of Artaxerxes the king, twelve years, neither I nor my brethren ate the food allowance of the governor. [15]The former governors who were before me laid heavy burdens upon the people, and took from them food and wine, besides forty shekels of silver. Even their servants lorded it over the people. But I did not do so, because of the fear of God. [16]I also held to the work on this wall, and acquired no land; and all my servants were gathered there for the work. [17]Moreover there were at my table a hundred and fifty men, Jews and officials, besides those who came to us from the nations which were about us. [18]Now that which was prepared for one day was one ox and six choice sheep; fowls likewise were prepared for me, and every ten days skins of wine in abundance; yet with all this I did not demand the food allowance of the governor, because the servitude was heavy upon this people. [19]Remember for my good, O my God, all that I have done for this people.

Nehemiah does not demand of the nobles something he was not prepared to do himself. Indeed, he had gone further and had not accepted the food allowance which was his due as governor. Though this is the first time he is mentioned as governor, he indicates that he was appointed as such right from the beginning of his commissioning "in the twentieth year of Artaxerxes" (cf. 2:1), that is 445 B.C. (see p. 181). The "former governors" could refer to Sheshbazzar and Zerubbabel to whom the same title is given (Ezra 5:14; Hag 1:1; 2:2) but, since the tone of Nehemiah's words is denunciatory, the "former governors" are more likely to be the officials of the province "Beyond the River" who had kept an eye on Judah before the time of Nehemiah. These were also entitled "governors" (Ezra 5:3; Neh 2:7).

Nehemiah must have had considerable private means if he was able to provide not only for his own household but also for all those who ate at his table in a display of true oriental hospitality. As well as officials and fellow Judeans, these included visitors from other lands which shows that Nehemiah's Jerusalem was as open politically as it was closed religiously. The list of good food and wines provided for his table would indicate that Nehemiah, for all his insistence on reform, had a zest for good living.

The chapter ends with a petition to God to remember to his good all that he had done for the welfare of the people. It is such notices (cf. 6:14; 13:14) which have given the impression of priggishness on the part of Nehemiah. But, as has been pointed out (see p. 178), they bear all the signs of statements in memorial inscriptions and so would be completely acceptable in ancient times.

PLOTS AND INTRIGUES CONTINUE
6:1-19

> **6** Now when it was reported to Sanballat and Tobiah and to Geshem the Arab and to the rest of our enemies that I had built the wall and that there was no breach left in it (although up to that time I had not set up the doors in the gates), ²Sanballat and Geshem sent to me, saying, "Come and let us meet together in one of the villages in the plain of Ono." But they intended to do me harm. ³And I sent messengers to them, saying, "I am doing a great work and I cannot come down. Why should the work stop while I leave it and come down to you?" ⁴And they sent to me four times in this way and I an-

swered them in the same manner. [5]In the same way
Sanballat for the fifth time sent his servant to me with an
open letter in his hand. [6]In it was written, "It is reported
among the nations, and Geshem also says it, that you and
the Jews intend to rebel; that is why you are building
the wall; and you wish to become their king, according
to this report. [7]And you have also set up prophets to
proclaim concerning you in Jerusalem, 'There is a king
in Judah.' And now it will be reported to the king according to these words. So now come, and let us take
counsel together." [8]Then I sent to him, saying, "No
such things as you say have been done, for you are in-
venting them out of your own mind." [9]For they all
wanted to frighten us, thinking, "Their hands will drop
from the work, and it will not be done." But now, O God,
strengthen thou my hands.

[10]Now when I went into the house of Shemaiah the son
of Delaiah, son of Mehetabel, who was shut up, he said,
"Let us meet together in the house of God, within the
temple, and let us close the doors of the temple; for they
are coming to kill you, at night they are coming to kill
you." [11]But I said, "Should such a man as I flee? And
what man such as I could go into the temple and live?
I will not go in." [12]And I understood, and saw that God
had not sent him, but he had pronounced the prophecy
against me because Tobiah and Sanballat had hired him.
[13]For this purpose he was hired, that I should be afraid
and act in this way and sin, and so they could give me
an evil name, in order to taunt me. [14]Remember Tobiah
and Sanballat, O my God, according to these things that
they did, and also the prophetess Noadiah and the rest of
the prophets who wanted to make me afraid.

[15]So the wall was finished on the twenty-fifth day of
the month Elul, in fifty-two days. [16]And when all our
enemies heard of it, all the nations round about us were
afraid and fell greatly in their own esteem; for they
perceived that this work had been accomplished with the
help of our God. [17]Moreover in those days the nobles of

Judah sent many letters to Tobiah, and Tobiah's letters came to them. [18]For many in Judah were bound by oath to him, because he was the son-in-law of Shecaniah the son of Arah; and his son Jehohanan had taken the daughter of Meshullam the son of Berechiah as his wife. [19]Also they spoke of his good deeds in my presence, and reported my words to him. And Tobiah sent letters to make me afraid.

This chapter follows on from the account of Nehemiah's opponents in chapter four. Because the rebuilding was succeeding beyond all expectations they shifted their efforts from hindering the work to attempting to get rid of Nehemiah altogether. The first attempt (vv.2-4) seems to have been an outright assassination plot under the pretence of making a treaty of peace. In the second (vv.5-8), they pretended to be giving friendly advice but in reality were spreading harmful rumours with a view to besmirching his reputation in the eyes of the Persians. They tried to suggest that he was about to set himself up as king in the style of the Northern Kingdom of old of having a prophet proclaim a new king (cf. 1 Kings 11:29-40). Haggai and Zechariah may have tried to do this for Zerubbabel (see p. 162). Nehemiah does not buy their endeavours and is also able for their next attempt (vv. 10-14).

At first sight this would seem to have been a genuine word from God but its contents are easily seen through by Nehemiah. The prophet, warning about an assassination plot which would presumably take place that very night, suggests that he hide in the inner sanctuary of the Temple. This would have had the effect of discrediting him on two counts. Firstly, there would be a slight on his personal bravery by suggesting that he would run away from danger. The second reason would be even more important: that as a layman he would dare to enter the inner sanctuary of the Temple (cf. 2 Chron 26:16-21). Nehemiah realises that the prophet is a hired man. His coolheadedness wins the day and he prays that his enemies' plots will recoil on their own heads. Such vindictiveness was part and parcel of the prayer of the time and can be found in many of the psalms (e.g. Ps 109[108]). It is understandable in the circumstances but has to be balanced by later insights into love of one's enemies.

A notice about the completion of the walls follows. It seems incredible that they should have been finished within the space of fifty-two days against such odds and, indeed, later sources are more realistic. Josephus, for instance, records that it took two years and four months to rebuild the walls. The month mentioned, *Elul*, corresponds to our August-September. The hand of God is seen in the favourable outcome and the opposition of Nehemiah's enemies is discredited. But they are not silenced and, indeed, band together with enemies from within - the same nobles who would have been dissatisfied with Nehemiah's reform measures and who were interrelated with Tobiah, one of the ringleaders of the opposition.

PEOPLING THE CITY
7:1-73

7 Now when the wall had been built and I had set up the doors, and the gatekeepers, the singers, and the Levites had been appointed, 2I gave my brother Hanani and Hananiah the governor of the castle charge over Jerusalem, for he was a more faithful and God-fearing man than many. 3And I said to them, "Let not the gates of Jerusalem be opened until the sun is hot; and while they are still standing guard let them shut and bar the doors. Appoint guards from among the inhabitants of Jerusalem, each to his station and each opposite his own house." 4The city was wide and large, but the people within it were few and no houses had been built.

5Then God put it into my mind to assemble the nobles and the officials and the people to be enrolled by genealogy. And I found the book of the genealogy of those

who came up at the first, and I found written in it:
⁶These were the people of the province who came up out of the captivity of those exiles whom Nebuchadnezzar the king of Babylon had carried into exile; they returned to Jerusalem and Judah, each to his town. ⁷They came with Zerubbabel, Jeshua, Nehemiah, Azariah, Raamiah, Nahamani, Mordecai, Bilshan, Mispereth, Bigvai, Nehum, Baanah.

Organisation of security personnel comes next - especially the gatekeepers. Automatically when these are mentioned the Chronicler adds in: "Singers and Levites." Nehemiah places trusted associates over all, his brother, Hanani, and Hananiah the governor of the castle. He orders that the gates be not opened until late in the morning and, presumably, shut before nightfall, though this latter notice does not appear in the text. As well as the official police force, he organises a kind of vigilante group who would guard around their own quarters.

Accommodation, however, was sparse so his next step was to rebuild houses and repeople the city now that it was secure to live there again. Following on the Nehemiah Memoirs is the same list which was presented in Ezra 2, providing a good example of how genealogies could be used for different purposes. There the list was used to show the continuity of history through the Exile; here it is the starting point of a campaign to induce those who had settled elsewhere to move to Jerusalem. The Memoirs then break off to reappear again throughout Neh 12 and 13.

IV. CEREMONIES AND REFORMS OF EZRA AND NEHEMIAH
Neh 8:1—13:31

IT IS USUALLY SUGGESTED that Nehemiah 8 originally followed the material contained in Ezra 8, since both sections are dealing with Ezra. The first part of the Nehemiah Memoirs would then be an interpolation. But there is also the possibility that this section is a deliberate arrangement of material about Ezra to parallel the earlier material (see p. 147). Again theological order takes precedence over chronological.

The section as it stands is the culmination of the founding events of post-exilic times. Just as the first founding of the Temple and the building-up of the community was established and confirmed by cultic ceremonies, so the same must be true for this new departure. There are some differences, however. The post-exilic emphasis on the importance of the Law is reflected in the ceremony of the reading of the Law being placed first in the order of ceremonial events. Eventually the reading of the Law in synagogues would take over from the sacrifices of the Temple.

THE READING OF THE LAW
7:73 - 8:18

.[73]And when the seventh month had come, the children of Israel were in their towns.

8 ¹And all the people gathered as one man into the square before the Water Gate; and they told Ezra the scribe to bring the book of the law of Moses which the Lord had given to Israel. ²And Ezra the priest brought the law before the assembly, both men and women and all who could hear with understanding, on the first day of the seventh month. ³And he read from it facing the square before the Water Gate from early morning until midday, in the presence of the men and the women and those who could understand; and the ears of all the people were attentive to the book of the law. ⁴And Ezra the scribe stood on a wooden pulpit which they had made for the purpose; and beside him stood Mattithiah, Shema, Anaiah, Uriah, Hilkiah, and Maaseiah on his right hand; and Pedaiah, Mishael, Malchijah, Hashum, Hashbaddanah, Zechariah, and Meshullam on his left hand. ⁵And Ezra opened the book in the sight of all the people, for he was above all the people; and when he opened it all the people stood. ⁶And Ezra blessed the Lord, the great God; and all the people answered, "Amen, Amen," lifting up their hands; and they bowed their heads and worshiped the Lord with their faces to the ground. ⁷Also Jeshua, Bani, Sherebiah, Jamin, Akkub, Shabbethai, Hodiah, Maaseiah, Kelita, Azariah, Jozabad, Hanan, Pelaiah, the Levites, helped the people to understand the law, while the people remained in their places. ⁸And they read from the book, from the law of God, clearly; and they gave the sense, so that the people understood the reading.

The events to follow in chapter eight take place in "the seventh month" (7:7). There were a number of reasons why the seventh month is mentioned. It was the feast month, par excellence, being the month in which the Day of Atonement was kept (but see p. 200) and the Feast of Tabernacles (cf. 8:13-18). The Ark was moved from Zion to the Temple at the feast of the seventh month in 2 Chronicles (cf. 5:3) and it was also in the seventh month that the people assembled at Jerusalem and made offerings before the foundations of the Temple were laid (Ezra 3:1,6).

The ceremony of the reading of the Law takes place not in the Temple but in a square of the city and it is read in the presence of all the people, men, women and even children who "could hear with understanding" (cf. Deut 30:2). The content of the book of the Law may have been the Pentateuch as we know it, though this has been disputed, since some sections of these chapters give regulations according to the code of Deuteronomy and do not seem to know the adaptations of the Priestly Code. At any rate Ezra did not read the whole book but only "from it" as he stood on a raised platform facing the people. The ceremony begins with the solemn blessing of God to which the people answer the "Amen" in a solemn attitude of prayer, lifting up their hands and then bowing with their faces to the ground. It is an attitude of prayer common among Muslims to this day.

Associated with Ezra in the reading of the Law are the Levites whose teaching functions are emphasised (see Intro. p. 5, 6). What exactly their function was on this occasion is difficult to determine since the text of 8:8 is far from self-evident. The word translated "clearly" in the RSV above could mean "with interpretation," as the RSV notes in the margin. But does this mean "translation" and imply a translation from Hebrew into Aramaic as the spoken language of the people of the time? The Jewish word for translations is *targum* and the Rabbis would later see the origins of these targums in this passage. But historically it is not at all evident that Aramaic had become the vernacular this early and at any rate there are other possible meanings to our text. "With interpretation" could also mean that the Levites in this case were engaged in applying the meaning of the Law to the lives of the people at that time. Still another possibility is that the word translated as "clearly" meant "split-up"; this would imply that the Levites took the Law section by section and explained it.

At the beginning of the sentence the words "they read" could also have been, "he (Ezra) read." The process which emerges from all this would seem to have been that Ezra read while the Levites interpreted the Law as best they could to the people.

CELEBRATIONS
8:9 - 9:5

⁹And Nehemiah, who was the governor, and Ezra the priest and scribe, and the Levites who taught the people said to all the people, "This day is holy to the Lord your God; do not mourn or weep." For all the people wept when they heard the words of the law. ¹⁰Then he said to them, "Go your way, eat the fat and drink sweet wine and send portions to him for whom nothing is prepared; for this day is holy to our Lord; and do not be grieved, for the joy of the Lord is your strength." ¹¹So the Levites stilled all the people, saying, "Be quiet, for this day is holy; do not be grieved." ¹²And all the people went their way to eat and drink and to send portions and to make great rejoicing, because they had understood the words that were declared to them.

¹³On the second day the heads of fathers' houses of all the people, with the priests and the Levites, came together to Ezra the scribe in order to study the words of the law. ¹⁴And they found it written in the law that the Lord had commanded by Moses that the people of Israel should dwell in booths during the feast of the seventh month, ¹⁵and that they should publish and proclaim in all their towns and in Jerusalem, "Go out to the hills and bring branches of olive, wild olive, myrtle, palm, and other leafy trees to make booths, as it is written." ¹⁶So the people went out and brought them and made booths for themselves, each on his roof, and in their courts and in the courts of the house of God, and in the square at the Water Gate and in the square at the Gate of

Ephraim. [17]And all the assembly of those who had
returned from the captivity made booths and dwelt in the
booths; for from the days of Jeshua the son of Nun to that
day the people of Israel had not done so. And there was
very great rejoicing. [18]And day by day, from the first day
to the last day, he read from the book of the law of God.
They kept the feast seven days; and on the eighth day
there was a solemn assembly, according to the ordinance.
9 Now on the twenty-fourth day of this month the
people of Israel were assembled with fasting and in sackcloth, and with earth upon their heads. [2]And the Israelites
separated themselves from all foreigners, and stood and
confessed their sins and the iniquities of their fathers.
[3]And they stood up in their place and read from the book
of the law of the Lord their God for a fourth of the day;
for another fourth of it they made confession and worshiped the Lord their God.

Nehemiah's name has probably been inserted in this passage to ensure that the governor would be seen to endorse
the reading of the Law. (That it is an insertion can be
judged from the fact that the verbs are in the singular and
that, therefore, Ezra's was the only name original to the
text.) The reaction of the people is first of all one of
mourning because they realise that they have not kept the
precepts of the Law, but Ezra insists that it is rather a time
for rejoicing. They were to show their joy by feasting and
drinking but also by sharing with those who were in need
(cf. Deut 16:14). That there was ignorance of the Law at
the time is clearly shown by the fact that the people did not
even know about the feast of Booths. Originally this had
been an agricultural feast to celebrate the ingathering of
the harvest (Deut 16:13-15). But in later times it was
connected with Israel's own peculiar history as a commem-
oration of the fact that they lived in booths during their
time of wandering in the desert (Lev 23:43). It is an exag-
geration to say, however, that the feast was not known since
the "days of Jeshua, the son of Nun," since there is mention

of it in Ezra 3, in the account of the attempts to rebuild the Temple (cf. 2 Chron 5:3; 7:8).

The feast was in the seventh month, the month especially devoted to feasts (see p. 196), but also appropriate as the month of the harvest. The Jewish calendar also kept the opposite kind of ceremony in the seventh month: the Day of Atonement (cf. Lev 23:27). There is no mention of its ritual here but there is a day of solemn penance which fulfils the same purpose: the people confess their sins and pray for forgiveness. Most commentators would like to reverse the order, putting the penance service before that of joy. This would be the logical order, of course, but by now one does not expect logical order in the books of Ezra and Nehemiah. The fact that it was placed first emphasises that the service of joy was considered a more fitting reaction to the reading of the Law than that of penance.

EZRA'S PRAYER
9:6-37

[6]And Ezra said: "Thou art the Lord, thou alone; thou hast made heaven, the heaven of heavens, with all their host, the earth and all that is on it, the seas and all that is in them; and thou preservest all of them; and the host of heaven worships thee. [7]Thou art the Lord, the God who didst choose Abram and bring him forth out of Ur of the Chaldeans and give him the name Abraham; [8]and thou didst find his heart faithful before thee, and didst make with him the covenant to give to his descendants the land of the Canaanite, the Hittite, the Amorite, the Perizzite, the Jebusite, and the Girgashite; and thou hast fulfilled thy promise, for thou art righteous.

[9]"And thou didst see the affliction of our fathers in Egypt and hear their cry at the Red Sea, [10]and didst perform signs and wonders against Pharaoh and all his servants and all the people of his land, for thou knewest that they acted insolently against our fathers; and thou

didst get thee a name, as it is to this day. [11]And thou didst divide the sea before them, so that they went through the midst of the sea on dry land; and thou didst cast their pursuers into the depths, as a stone into mighty waters. [12]By a pillar of cloud thou didst lead them in the day, and by a pillar of fire in the night to light for them the way in which they should go. [13]Thou didst come down upon Mount Sinai, and speak with them from heaven and give them right ordinances and true laws, good statutes and commandments, [14]and thou didst make known to them thy holy sabbath and command them commandments and statutes and a law by Moses thy servant. [15]Thou didst give them bread from heaven for their hunger and bring forth water for them from the rock for their thirst, and thou didst tell them to go in to possess the land which thou hadst sworn to give them. . . .

[26]"Nevertheless they were disobedient and rebelled against thee and cast thy law behind their back and killed thy prophets, who had warned them in order to turn them back to thee, and they committed great blasphemies. [27]Therefore thou didst give them into the hand of their enemies, who made them suffer; and in the time of their suffering they cried to thee and thou didst hear them from heaven; and according to thy great mercies thou didst give them saviors who saved them from the hand of their enemies. [28]But after they had rest they did evil again before thee, and thou didst abandon them to the hand of their enemies, so that they had dominion over them; yet when they turned and cried to thee thou didst hear from heaven, and many times thou didst deliver them according to thy mercies. . . .

[32]"Now therefore, our God, the great and mighty and terrible God, who keepest covenant and steadfast love, let not all the hardship seem little to thee that has come upon us, upon our kings, our princes, our priests, our prophets, our fathers, and all thy people, since the time of the kings of Assyria until this day. [33]Yet thou hast been just in all that has come upon us, for thou

hast dealt faithfully and we have acted wickedly; [34]our kings, our princes, our priests, and our fathers have not kept thy law or heeded thy commandments and thy warnings which thou didst give them. [35]They did not serve thee in their kingdom, and in thy great goodness which thou gavest them, and in the large and rich land which thou didst set before them; and they did not turn from their wicked works. [36]Behold, we are slaves this day; in the land that thou gavest to our fathers to enjoy its fruit and its good gifts, behold, we are slaves. [37]And its rich yield goes to the kings whom thou hast set over us because of our sins; they have power also over our bodies and over our cattle at their pleasure, and we are in great distress."

The prayer in Nehemiah 9 centres around the past action of God's covenanted grace and love towards his people, stressing his continual fidelity in spite of their constant apostasy. This fidelity would remain with them into the future if they would only renew their covenant with God. The prayer is therefore linked with the covenant which follows rather than with the penitential rite which preceeds the passage. Perhaps there was a shorter penitential prayer here originally. In contrast to similar calls in Chronicles (cf. 1 Chron 28:8; 2 Chron 7:17), the basis of this covenant between God and the people is that concluded in the time of the Exodus and Sinai rather than that with David (see Intro. p. 4).

Prayers are often used in Chronicles as a method of instruction and exhortation (cf. 1 Chron 29:10-19; 2 Chron 20:6-12) but this one has more in common with passages outside Chronicles-Ezra-Nehemiah than with anything within. For this reason many scholars would consider the prayer as an insertion into the text. As it stands it seems a deliberate parallel to Ezra 9 (see p. 148).

The prayer itself is a mosaic of quotations from earlier passages of the Bible. (The list of parallels are set out in more lengthy commentaries and run to three or four pages.)

The result, however, is not merely a string of quotations but a new theological expression skillfully woven from many earlier insights. It is an example of what the Rabbis would later call "stringing pearls." Each pearl of Scripture is beautiful in its own setting but when its meaning is pierced and linked with others of value, the completed necklace has a power and a beauty which surpasses the sum of each individual piece. The prayer of Nehemiah 9 has to be viewed in some such fashion.

THE COVENANT
9:38-10:39

[38]Because of all this we make a firm covenant and write it, and our princes, our Levites, and our priests set their seal to it.
10 Those who set their seal are Nehemiah the governor, the son of Hacaliah, Zedekiah, [2]Seraiah, Azariah, Jeremiah, [3]Pashhur, Amariah, Malchijah, [4]Hattush, Shebaniah, Malluch,...
[28]The rest of the people, the priests, the Levites, the gatekeepers, the singers, the temple servants, and all who have separated themselves from the peoples of the lands to the law of God, their wives, their sons, their daughters, all who have knowledge and understanding, [29]join with their brethren, their nobles, and enter into a curse and an oath to walk in God's law which was given by Moses the servant of God, and to observe and do all the commandments of the Lord our Lord and his ordinances and his statutes. [30]We will not give our daughters to the peoples of the land or take their daughters for our sons; [31]and if the peoples of the land bring in wares or any grain on the sabbath day to sell, we will not buy from them on the sabbath or on a holy day; and we will forego the crops of the seventh year and the exaction of every debt.
[32]We also lay upon ourselves the obligation to charge ourselves yearly with the third part of a shekel for the

service of the house of our God; [33]for the show-bread, the continual cereal offering, the continual burnt offering, the sabbaths, the new moons, the appointed feasts, the holy things, and the sin offerings to make atonement for Israel, and for all the work of the house of our God. [34]We have likewise cast lots, the priests, the Levites, and the people, for the wood offering, to bring it into the house of our God, according to our fathers' houses, at times appointed, year by year, to burn upon the altar of the Lord our God, as it is written in the law. [35]We obligate ourselves to bring the first fruits of our ground and the first fruits of all fruit of every tree, year by year, to the house of the Lord; [36]also to bring to the house of our God, to the priests who minister in the house of our God, the first-born of our sons and of our cattle, as it is written in the law, and the firstlings of our herds and of our flocks; [37]and to bring the first of our coarse meal, and our contributions, the fruit of every tree, the wine and the oil, to the priests, to the chambers of the house of our God; and to bring to the Levites the tithes from our ground, for it is the Levites who collect the tithes in all our rural towns. [38]And the priest, the son of Aaron, shall be with the Levites when the Levites receive the tithes; and the Levites shall bring up the tithe of the tithes to the house of our God, to the chambers, to the storehouse. [39]For the people of Israel and the sons of Levi shall bring the contribution of grain, wine, and oil to the chambers, where are the vessels of the sanctuary, and the priests that minister, and the gatekeepers and the singers. We will not neglect the house of our God.

The picture presented in chapter ten is of the ideal post-exilic community covenanted to God as a holy people and gathered around his Temple. It can be looked on as an ideal conclusion, in the eyes of the Chronicler, to the work both of Ezra and of Nehemiah. It is presented in the form of a legal document signed and sealed by the leading men of the time, both priestly and lay. The list is headed by Nehemiah as governor. It is perhaps again a list taken from Temple archives. Many earlier aspects of covenant-making re-appear. such as the solemn oath-taking ceremony (vv. 28-29) which bound the people to carry out the injunctions of the covenant (cf. Deut 27), but the contents deal with the specific problems of post-exilic times. Many of these reappear in chapter thirteen where Nehemiah's efforts to deal with them are outlined.

The first, and most persistent, problem was the question of intermarriage with foreigners which has already been discussed. It is interesting to note that the people are not ordered to break up existing marriages here but to refrain from entering into new ones. The next question dealt with was that of keeping the Sabbath holy. The original reason for the prohibition of work on the Sabbath was probably, in a rural set-up, to ensure that servants and slaves had some rest in the week (cf. Deut 5:12-15). Here it is to ensure the holiness of the covenanted community (cf. Ex 20:8-11). The purpose of allowing the land to go fallow every seven years also probably had a common sense reason behind it: the land cannot be worked to death. It could also be related to provision for the poor which was a feature of the reform of Nehemiah. Concern for the poor is further stressed by the injunction to remit debts every seven years.

The remainder of the legislation deals with the thorny problem of the upkeep of the sanctuary and so relates directly to the Chronicler's vision of a people at peace, worshipping God in a well-ordered sanctuary and with a well-directed liturgy. Priests and Levites could perform their duties efficiently because tithes and offerings flowed in on a regular basis. The final word of the covenant, "We will not neglect the house of our God," could be the theme song of the Chronicler's whole work.

JERUSALEM REPEOPLED
11:1-12:26

11 Now the leaders of the people lived in Jerusalem, and the rest of the people cast lots to bring one out of ten to live in Jerusalem the holy city, while nine tenths remained in the other towns. [2]And the people blessed all the men who willingly offered to live in Jerusalem.

[3]These are the chiefs of the province who lived in Jerusalem; but in the towns of Judah every one lived on his property in their towns: Israel, the priests, the Levites, the temple servants, and the descendants of Solomon's servants. [4]And in Jerusalem lived certain of the sons of Judah and of the sons of Benjamin....

[25]And as for the villages, with their fields, some of the people of Judah lived in Kiriatharba and its villages, and in Dibon and its villages, and in Jekabzeel and its villages, [26]and in Jeshua and in Moladah and Bethpelet....

12   These are the priests and the Levites who came up with Zerubbabel the son of Shealtiel, and Jeshua: Seraiah, Jeremiah, Ezra, [2]Amariah, Malluch, Hattush, [3]Shecaniah, Rehum, Meremoth, [4]Iddo, Ginnethoi, Abijah, [5]Mijamin, Maadiah, Bilgah, [6]Shemaiah, Joiarib, Jedaiah, [7]Sallu, Amok, Hilkiah, Jedaiah. These were the chiefs of the priests and of their brethren in the days of Jeshua.

[8]And the Levites: Jeshua, Binnui, Kadmiel, Sherebiah, Judah, and Mattaniah, who with his brethren was in charge of the songs of thanksgiving. [9]And Bakbukiah and Unno their brethren stood opposite them in the service. [10]And Jeshua was the father of Joiakim, Joiakim the father of Eliashib, Eliashib the father of Joiada, [11]Joiada the father of Jonathan, and Jonathan the father of Jaddua....

[22]As for the Levites, in the days of Eliashib, Joiada, Johanan, and Jaddua, there were recorded the heads of fathers' houses; also the priests until the reign of Darius the Persian. [23]The sons of Levi, heads of fathers' houses, were written in the Book of the Chronicles until the days of Johanan the son of Eliashib. [24]And the chiefs of the Levites: Hashabiah, Sherebiah, and Jeshua the son of Kadmiel, with their brethren over against them, to praise

and to give thanks, according to the commandment of David the man of God, watch corresponding to watch. [25]Mattaniah, Bakbukiah, Obadiah, Meshullam, Talmon, and Akkub were gatekeepers standing guard at the storehouses of the gates. [26]These were in the days of Joiakim the son of Jeshua son of Jozadak, and in the days of Nehemiah the governor and of Ezra the priest the scribe.

Creativity in the use of lists and genealogies is as much a feature of this section as it was of the first nine chapters of Chronicles and of other passages in Ezra-Nehemiah (cf. Ezra 2; Neh 12:1-26). In fact the suspicion lingers (now that all of them have been examined) that the same lists, with extensions and omissions, form the basis of many of the passages. Much of what is given here for the repeopling of the city was used to advantage in 1 Chronicles 9 (see p.24) as a link between Israel's past and present and in Ezra 2 (cf. Neh 7) as a list of the returning exiles. Creativity in the use of statistics is not just a feature of the present age as has been pointed out (see p. 13).

Unlike our age, however, where the population of a country drifts in towards the cities from rural areas, there was a marked hesitation on the part of the people of Judah to repopulate the city of Jerusalem after the walls had been repaired. So much so that those who allowed their names to go forward for the drawing of lots were considered very patriotic. A tenth of the population was to be selected. This has obvious cultic connotations; just as a tenth of the produce and flocks were to be set aside as a dedication to God (cf. Amos 4:4; Mal 3:8), so a tenth of the population were to people the holy city. The city is here called the "holy city," a name increasingly given to it in the postexilic period (cf. Is 48:2). Probably originally the presence of God which the title implies was confined to the "holy of holies," then, by extension, the title was given to the Temple as a whole and finally to the city itself. This idea is reflected today in the Arabic name for Jerusalem: *el quds* (the holy).

Among the lists given in this section is one of the towns and villages of Judah in which the people lived. There is controversy as to whether this represents the actual historical situation in the post-exilic period. Some of the villages mentioned, for instance Beerarabah and Beersheba, seem a bit too far south to be included in the territory of Nehemiah's governorship, since there is evidence to suggest that the hill region south of Hebron was not included in the province of Judah. Hebron is less than twenty miles south of Jerusalem whereas Beersheba would be over forty.

A list which is very important historically is that of the high priests in the post-exilic period (12:10-11; cf. v.23). This appears to give the genealogy of the high priests from the time of the rebuilding of the Temple under Zerubbabel (Ezra 4) until at least the time of Darius II (423-404). This list is one of the primary reasons why some think that Nehemiah came before Ezra since Nehemiah was contemporary with Eliashib, third on the list (cf. Neh 3:1; 13:4) and Ezra presumably with Jonathan, fifth on the list (cf. Ezra 10:6). On the other hand, it has been pointed out that there is too big a gap in time between the first and third high priest (520 B.C. - 445 B.C.) which could not possibly have been filled by one man, Joiakim. For this reason, and working from contemporary documents, an earlier Johanan has been posited who would have been contemporary with the earlier date for Ezra in 458 B.C. This seemed a reasonable solution when it was first put forward but it has not solved all the problems. As was pointed out earlier, the relation of Ezra to Nehemiah and the relative dates of each still remains one of the greatest puzzles in biblical scholarship.

THE DEDICATION OF THE CITY WALLS
12:27-47

27And at the dedication of the wall of Jerusalem they sought the Levites in all their places, to bring them to

Jerusalem to celebrate the dedication with gladness, with thanksgivings and with singing, with cymbals, harps, and lyres. [28]And the sons of the singers gathered together from the circuit round Jerusalem.

[30]And the priests and the Levites purified themselves; and they purified the people and the gates and the wall.

[31]Then I brought up the princes of Judah upon the wall, and appointed two great companies which gave thanks and went in procession. One went to the right upon the wall to the Dung Gate; [32]and after them went Hoshaiah and half of the princes of Judah, [33]and Azariah, Ezra, Meshullam, [34]Judah, Benjamin, Shemaiah, and Jeremiah, [35]and certain of the priests' sons with trumpets: Zechariah the son of Jonathan, son of Shemaiah, son of Mattaniah, son of Micaiah, son of Zaccur, son of Asaph; [36]and his kinsmen, Shemaiah, Azarel, Milalai, Gilalai, Maai, Nethanel, Judah, and Hanani, with the musical instruments of David the man of God; and Ezra the scribe went before them. [37]At the Fountain Gate they went up straight before them by the stairs of the city of David, at the ascent of the wall, above the house of David, to the Water Gate on the east.

[38]The other company of those who gave thanks went to the left, and I followed them with half of the people, upon the wall, above the Tower of the Ovens, to the Broad Wall, [39]and above the Gate of Ephraim, and by the Old Gate, and by the Fish Gate and the Tower of Hananel and the Tower of the Hundred, to the Sheep Gate; and they came to a halt at the Gate of the Guard. [40]So both companies of those who gave thanks stood in the house of God, and I and half of the officials with me; [41]and the priests Eliakim, Maaseiah, Miniamin, Micaiah, Elioenai, Zechariah, and Hananiah, with trumpets; [42]and Maaseiah, Shemaiah, Eleazar, Uzzi, Jahohanan, Malchijah, Elam, and Ezer. And the singers sang with Jezrahiah as their leader. [43]And they offered great sacrifices that day and rejoiced, for God had made them rejoice with great joy; the women and children also rejoiced. And the

joy of Jerusalem was heard afar off.

⁴⁴On that day men were appointed over the chambers for the stores, the contributions, the first fruits, and the tithes, to gather into them the portions required by the law for the priests and for the Levites according to the fields of the towns; for Judah rejoiced over the priests and the Levites who ministered. ⁴⁵And they performed the service of their God and the service of purification, as did the singers and the gatekeepers, according to the command of David and his son Solomon. ⁴⁶For in the days of David and Asaph of old there was a chief of the singers, and there were songs of praise and thanksgiving to God. ⁴⁷And all Israel in the days of Zerubbabel and in the days of Nehemiah gave the daily portions for the singers and the gatekeepers; and they set apart that which was for the Levites; and the Levites set apart that which was for the sons of Aaron.

The Nehemiah Memoirs are used again for the description of the solemn dedication of the city walls, another of the great ceremonies outlined in this part of the books of Ezra and Nehemiah. It is carried out with all due ceremony and so the presence of the Levites, singers and gatekeepers is prominent. The ceremony begins with purification - of the people and of the gates and walls. Then a solemn procession is organised. The unusual feature of this procession is that it is split in half, each half consisting of a choir, an official of high rank, half of the family heads, priests and Levites. The presence of Ezra as one of the officials has been seen as a deliberate insertion into the Nehemiah material, again evidence of the tendency to parallel the two great leaders (see p. 148).

Each half of the procession would do a half circle of the walls until they met again in the Temple. The first group went south; the second north. This type of split procession has reappeared down the ages in religious worship, for example in the Philippines during Holy Week, where the women follow the statue of the Mother of Sorrows and the men that of the Crucified and both sides meet again in the church for solemn ceremonies.

When the two halves of the procession reunite on this occasion in the Temple, great sacrifices are offered and the people rejoice "with great joy" (cf. Ezra 3:11). It is stated that the "joy of Jerusalem was heard afar off" which is not merely a notice about the amount of noise they could muster up but, rather, a call to the nations to share their joy at what God had done for his people.

The end of the chapter presents a typical schema of what a well-ordered and smooth-functioning Temple should be like (see p. 148). The Temple would have its full complement of priests, Levites, singers and gatekeepers; the taxes and tithes would be paid with joy by the people while each group of functionaries would pass on its share to the group above them; the singing guilds would perform as laid down for them in the past. The picture is idyllic rather than actual as chapter thirteen will go on to point out.

NEHEMIAH'S SECOND TERM AS GOVERNOR
13:1-31

13 On that day they read from the book of Moses in the hearing of the people; and in it was found written that no Ammonite or Moabite should ever enter the assembly of God; ²for they did not meet the children of Israel with bread and water, but hired Balaam against them to curse them—yet our God turned the curse into a blessing. ³When the people heard the law, they separated from Israel all those of foreign descent.

⁴Now before this, Eliashib the priest, who was appointed over the chambers of the house of our God, and who was connected with Tobiah, ⁵prepared for Tobiah a large chamber where they had previously put the cereal offering, the frankincense, the vessels, and the tithes of grain, wine, and oil, which were given by commandment to the Levites, singers, and gatekeepers, and the contri-

butions for the priests. [6]While this was taking place I was not in Jerusalem, for in the thirty-second year of Artaxerxes king of Babylon I went to the king. And after some time I asked leave of the king [7]and came to Jerusalem, and I then discovered the evil that Eliashib had done for Tobiah, preparing for him a chamber in the courts of the house of God. [8]And I was very angry, and I threw all the household furniture of Tobiah out of the chamber. [9]Then I gave orders and they cleansed the chambers; and I brought back thither the vessels of the house of God, with the cereal offering and the frankincense.

[10]I also found out that the portions of the Levites had not been given to them; so that the Levites and the singers, who did the work, had fled each to his field. [11]So I remonstrated with the officials and said, "Why is the house of God forsaken?" And I gathered them together and set them in their stations. [12]Then all Judah brought the tithe of the grain, wine, and oil into the storehouses . . . .

[15]In those days I saw in Judah men treading wine presses on the sabbath, and bringing in heaps of grain and loading them on asses; and also wine, grapes, figs, and all kinds of burdens, which they brought into Jerusalem on the sabbath day; and I warned them on the day when they sold food. [16]Men of Tyre also, who lived in the city, brought in fish and all kinds of wares and sold them on the sabbath to the people of Judah, and in Jerusalem. [17]Then I remonstrated with the nobles of Judah and said to them, "What is this evil thing which you are doing, profaning the sabbath day? [18]Did not your fathers act in this way, and did not our God bring all this evil on us and on this city? Yet you bring more wrath upon Israel by profaning the sabbath."

[19]When it began to be dark at the gates of Jerusalem before the sabbath, I commanded that the doors should be shut and gave orders that they should not be opened until after the sabbath. And I set some of my servants over the gates, that no burden might be brought in on the

sabbath day. [20]Then the merchants and sellers of all kinds of wares lodged outside Jerusalem once or twice. [21]But I warned them and said to them, "Why do you lodge before the wall? If you do so again I will lay hands on you." From that time on they did not come on the sabbath. [22]And I commanded the Levites that they should purify themselves and come and guard the gates, to keep the sabbath day holy. Remember this also in my favor, O my God, and spare me according to the greatness of thy steadfast love.

[23]In those days also I saw the Jews who had married women of Ashdod, Ammon, and Moab; [24]and half of their children spoke the language of Ashdod, and they could not speak the language of Judah, but the language of each people. [25]And I contended with them and cursed them and beat some of them and pulled out their hair; and I made them take oath in the name of God, saying, "You shall not give your daughters to their sons, or take their daughters for your sons or for yourselves. [26]Did not Solomon king of Israel sin on account of such women? Among the many nations there was no king like him, and he was beloved by his God, and God made him king over all Israel; nevertheless foreign women made even him to sin. [27]Shall we then listen to you and do all this great evil and act treacherously against our God by marrying foreign women?"

[28]And one of the sons of Jehoiada, the son of Eliashib the high priest, was the son-in-law of Sanballat the Horonite; therefore I chased him from me. [29]Remember them, O my God, because they have defiled the priesthood and the covenant of the priesthood and the Levites.

[30]Thus I cleansed them from everything foreign, and I established the duties of the priests and Levites, each in his work; [31]and I provided for the wood offering, at appointed times, and for the first fruits. Remember me, O my God, for good.

It is tempting to think that the books of Ezra and Nehemiah once ended with chapter twelve. Certainly one would expect to be left with some such glowing picture of the happy state of affairs in Jerusalem where everything was running on oiled wheels and the whole people were joyfully centred around the Temple and its worship. The sour note of chapter thirteen with its chronicle of wrong-doing is an anti-climax. But it seems a deliberate one: a picture of how things should not be is a better warning to remain faithful, perhaps, than would be the rosy presentation of chapter twelve.

The section deals largely with Nehemiah's second term of office. During the interval of his return to the Persian court, a lax state of affairs emerged in Judah, symbolised by the permission given to Tobiah, Nehemiah's archenemy (cf. 2:10; 4:3), to lodge in the Temple precincts when he was in Jerusalem. The Temple itself appeared in a sorry state: the people were not paying their dues and so the Levites had disbanded and gone to seek a living elsewhere. Nehemiah remedied the situation as well as that of the violation of the Sabbath. Elsewhere in the Bible neglect of the Sabbath was looked on as a cause of the misfortune of the people (cf. Jer 17:19-27; Ezek 20:12-24). The complete disruption of Sabbath rest was, therefore, a signal for vigorous action on the part of Nehemiah. The gates of the city were shut to keep out the foreign traders and levitical guards posted at them.

But Nehemiah's greatest battleground was in the arena of mixed marriages, a problem which was again threatening the self-identity of the community (cf. Ezra 9). He noticed the effects first of all in the speech of the children who would naturally have picked up their mother's intonations. This angered him since language and self-identity are often closely akin. His reaction against these mixed marriages was violent in the extreme, especially when he realised that the family of the high priest was involved and that with the family of his other great enemy, Sanballat (cf. 2:10,19; 4:1). He draws the parallel with Solomon's foreign wives leading him into sin, a parallel which was not drawn in

Chronicles (cf. 2 Kings 11; 1 Chron 7:11; see p. 172). But Nehemiah does not go as far as Ezra in his condemnation of mixed marriages. He forbids the contraction of new marriages but he does not break up existing ones as Ezra did.

Nehemiah's final word is a recommendation of himself to God for his zeal in regard to Jerusalem and religious worship, in particular by purging the priesthood of abuses (see p. 178).

CONCLUSION

THERE IS A GRANDEUR and at the same time a narrowness about the books we have been considering; a grandeur because they present a vision of the greatness of human life in its relation to God and the world in spite of the puny conditions in which the people of post-exilic times lived out their existence. A narrowness, because they were in danger of limiting God to reacting in a mechanical way to the right and wrong practised by the people (Chronicles), or confining him to be their own exclusive possession (Ezra and Nehemiah). But if this particular stance of reinterpreting the past understanding of God had not been taken, perhaps the Jewish faith itself would not have survived.

No age has a monopoly of insight into God but each age has its own contribution to make to the full spectrum of human understanding of the divine. The place of these books on that spectrum may not provide the most colourful aspects, nor even the most appealing, yet if they were left out there would be a vital shade missing, a valuable insight lost forever.

FOR FURTHER READING

P. R. Ackroyd, *Exile and Restoration. A Study of Hebrew Thought of the Sixth Century B.C.* (Old Testament Library) London: SCM, 1968.
This is probably the classic treatment of the period in English.

P.R. Ackroyd, *I & II Chronicles, Ezra, Nehemiah* (Torch Bible Paperbacks), London: SCM, 1973
A readable introduction to the books.

Y. Aharoni, *The Land of the Bible*, London: Buns and Oates, 1967.
A valuable introduction to the historical geography of the land.

B. W. Anderson, *The Living World of the Old Testament*, London: Longmans, 1967 (second ed., reprinted pb. 1980), pp. 430-463.
A succinct chapter on the post-exilic period in one of the most readable introductions to the Bible.

R. L. Braun, "Chronicles, Ezra and Nehemiah: Theology and Literary History. Studies in the Historical Books of the Old Testaments," *Suppl. Vet. Test.* 30 (1979) pp. 52-64.
This article is a fine example of the ongoing scholarly debate on the books of Chronicles, Ezra and Nehemiah.

R. J. Coggins, *Samaritans and Jews: the Origins of Samaritanism Reconsidered*, Oxford: Blackwell, 1975.
A warning that the relationship between the two groups in the post-exilic period has been grossly over-simplified.

S. Japhet, "Chronicles, Book of," in, *Encyclopaedia Judaica*, Jerusalem: Keter Pub. House, 1971, vol. 5, cols. 517-534.
> For those who have access to this encyclopaedia, this article provides the best introduction to recent thinking on Chronicles.

M. D. Johnson, *The Purpose of the Biblical Genealogies* (Soc. for NT Studies. Monograph Series 8.), Cambridge: University Press, 1969.
> A definitive study on the use of genealogies in the Bible.

C. H. Miller, "Salvation History - An Interpretation Tool," *Bible Today* 100 (1979) 1874-1878 (see 1879-1900).
> The first of a series of articles which illustrate (among other things) the way in which earlier material was continually being reinterpreted within the Bible itself.

J. M. Myers, *I Chronicles* (Anchor Bible)
J.M. Myers, *II Chronicles* (Anchor Bible)
J.M. Myers, *Ezra, Nehemiah* (Anchor Bible), Garden City, New York: Doubleday, 1965.
> Thorough and detailed commentaries on the books but needing some updating in the light of recent research.

R. North, "1-2 Chronicles. Ezra and Nehemiah," *The Jerome Biblical Commentary*, Eaglewood Cliffs: Prentice-Hall, 1968.
> A concise treatment of the books; of particular value for those who need a commentary on individual sections.

D. L. Petersen, *Late Israelite Prophecy: Studies in Deutero-Prophetic Literature and in Chronicles*, Missoula, Montana: Scholar's Press, 1977.
> An important study of the way prophecy developed in post-exilic times and of the place of Chronicles in that development.

H. Swanston, *Scripture Discussion Commentary. Histories II*, London: Sheed and Ward, 1972.
>   A short readable commentary with discussion questions which attempt to apply the message of the books to the present day.

H. G. M. Williamson, *Israel in the Books of Chronicles,* Cambridge: Cambridge University Press, 1977.
>   A stimulating special study which question many of the presuppositions about the relation of Chronicles to Ezra and Nehemiah.